Praise for *First Impressions*

"Over the past year, I have had the pleasure of getting to know Matt off-camera. He is a lover of people, a servant of his community, and a man of faith. You may have met the man on-screen, but get to know the person, and a journey, that will move your heart and open your eyes to a life one could only imagine living."

—Emmanuel Acho, Emmy Award winner and *New York Times* bestselling author of *Uncomfortable Conversations with a Black Man*

"I thought I learned everything there is to know about Matt during quarantine...turns out I was wrong. He's such a great human and his book has something for EVERYONE. You will not regret buying this book!!"

—Hannah Brown, TV personality and *New York Times* bestselling author

"Matt bares his whole soul in this book. *First Impressions* is a moving and raw look into Matt's life, and I couldn't be more excited for the world to experience it."

—Suni Lee, Olympic gold medalist

"The real Matt is in between the pages of this book—complex, multi-faceted, complicated. You walk away from this book knowing so much more than you saw on-screen, and trust me, you won't be disappointed."

—Kenya Moore, TV personality

"Matt's willingness to be vulnerable, honest, and self-reflective about himself is a refreshing read and emblematic of the kind man he is and the buoyant spirit he has."

—Melora Hardin

"Matt James is one person that is not afraid to use his platform. During *The Bachelor* and *Dancing with the Stars*, the world got to see a glimpse of the many layers of MJ. This book will really let you behind the veil to see the struggle, everything he has faced and overcome. Through it all, he stays grounded in who he is and never loses sight of his purpose. I'm honored to call Matt a friend and a brother. Get ready for a book that has the power to bring us all together and help guide us to really start understanding each other."

—Jimmie Allen

First
Impressions

First Impressions

Off-Screen Conversations with a BACHELOR on Race, Family, and Forgiveness

Matt James

with Cole Brown

New York • Nashville

Copyright © 2022 by Matt James

Cover design by Micah Kandros. Cover photography © Micah Kandros. Cover copyright © 2022 by Hachette Book Group, Inc.

Worthy
Hachette Book Group
1290 Avenue of the Americas, New York, NY 10104
Worthy.com
twitter.com/Worthy

First Edition: May 2022

Worthy is a division of Hachette Book Group, Inc. The Worthy name and logo are trademarks of Hachette Book Group, Inc.

The publisher is not responsible for websites (or their content) that are not owned by the publisher.

The Hachette Speakers Bureau provides a wide range of authors for speaking events. To find out more, go to www.hachettespeakersbureau.com or call (866) 376-6591.

Unless otherwise indicated, scripture quotations are taken from The Holy Bible, New International Version® NIV® copyright © 1973, 1978, 1984, 2011 by Biblica, Inc.™. Used by permission. All rights reserved worldwide.

LCCN: 2021952446

ISBNs: 9781546002086 (hardcover), 9781546003007 (signed), 9781546002109 (ebook)

Printed in the United States of America

LSC-C

Printing 1, 2022

For my mother, Patty James

Contents

Foreword
by *New York Times* Bestselling Author
Emmanuel Acho

The summer of 2020 was one of the most divisive time periods in America's recent history. The murder of George Floyd forced America to focus on our ever-present racial divide. Thousands marched through the streets, and when they returned home, had the uncomfortable conversations on race that they'd long put off. In boardrooms, company officials repeated the same conversations families had in the dining room. Change followed. For the first time in my life, I saw consumers demand more than polite talk from the companies they supported. Nowhere was this clearer than the world I live and work in—Hollywood—where all at once, entertainment executives were forced to reexamine the narratives they project out into the world.

Few platforms were pressed as hard as *The Bachelor* franchise, and rightfully so. Forty seasons into America's favorite dating show, and my friend Rachel Lindsay was still the only Black person to ever have starred in a season. *Bachelor* alumni joined with fans, pressuring the show to choose differently. They used their platforms to speak out against the whitewashed narratives *The Bachelor* had long embraced. They called for Black love. And in June 2020, *The Bachelor*'s producers answered their calls. We learned from *Good Morning America* that, for the first time in *The Bachelor*'s eighteen-year history, a Black man would lead the franchise.

When I first heard the news, I had two instantaneous thoughts. The first was simply, "Wow, it took them long enough." Eighteen years is a long, long, long time. It was hard not to feel both encouraged and disappointed that we still have "first" anythings in 2020.

My second thought: "I hope this Black man represents himself, his family, and his community properly." Being the first comes with its own set of pressures. Black people aren't afforded the same margin for error as our white counterparts. Every Black *Bachelor* cast member after this man would be judged by his performance. And a whole group of Americans would learn about Black dignity, vulnerability, and love for the first time through his example.

As fate would have it, I had little to worry about. I found out this Black man's name was Matt James, and represent himself well in the midst of inexplicable turmoil is exactly what he did.

I met Matt the same way the rest of America did: on the TV screen. I recall him opening up his first episode with prayer. He made a strong first impression on me that day. The moment told me much of what I needed to know about the core of the man. I knew then that, regardless of the twists and turns in the season ahead, Matt's faith would guide him along the journey. His principled approach told me I could breathe easy; this brother had the goods.

Millions of people witnessed Matt's journey through the season that followed, but few will ever understand it. Being the Bachelor comes with an inherited set of stressors, particularly in this day and age of social media, when everyone has the ability to express their disapproval of every action you take. Despite the pressure, at every opportunity, Matt chose grace and courage. He displayed his truest self for dozens of women and millions of viewers to see and judge. He followed his heart to a woman he loved. He handled the well-trodden Bachelor journey as well as any man who came before him, but then came complexities that no one—not Matt, not America, not even *The Bachelor*'s producers—saw coming.

I don't need to retell the story of the racially insensitive pictures that surfaced during Matt's season and the controversy that followed. It's out there already, and this book is a space for Matt to give his own version of those events. What I will say is that, like many of you, I followed those events as they unfolded in real time. I sympathized with the difficult decisions Matt faced, pressures from white and Black viewers alike, often pointing in opposite directions. I was no less impressed with Matt on the day the season finale aired than I was on the day the season began. Without yet knowing him personally, I sensed his thoughtful approach to all the controversy mounting before him. He led with integrity and I respected him for it from afar.

As you likely already know, Matt wasn't the only one in *The Bachelor* universe that faced controversy during his season. The racial reckoning touched every corner of the franchise, including its longtime host. His midseason resignation left a hole to fill for the reunion show. Since beginning my career in public life, I have made it my mission to walk head-on into uncomfortable conversations on race. I've always believed that respectful confrontation—not polite avoidance—is the surest path to progress. I was asked to fill the former host's shoes because of my comfort with the uncomfortable. And if *anything* was certain, it was that the conversation ahead would be uncomfortable. A room filled with one Bachelor, more than a dozen ex-girlfriends, and the looming presence of race is enough to make any man squirm.

It's hard to believe now, given how close we have become, but I met Matt for the first time during our taping of *The Bachelor: After the Final Rose*. In some ways, like America, I felt I already knew him by then. He had shown so much of himself throughout the season. His first impression hadn't faded; I liked the guy, which only made the job ahead more difficult.

If I cheered for Matt privately, publicly, I had to ask him the hard questions. Much had happened in his life since the taping of the finale. The racially insensitive photos had surfaced. The former host had departed. Matt and Rachael had broken up. It was my job to push him to unpack this rollercoaster ride of successes, missteps, and regrets.

With more than seven million Americans watching, Matt had to navigate giving grace to a woman he had great affection for while simultaneously honoring himself. I understood the pressure he must've faced. No matter which way his heart leaned, if he was too quick to forgive, our own community would line up to criticize his choices. On the largest stage imaginable, he had to process through high-profile heartbreak in real time. I asked him the tough questions and he answered every one with dignity and compassion in the midst of his own brokenness.

On camera, there was a noticeable distance between Rachael and him. What America didn't see was that, when the cameras stopped rolling and the lights dimmed, they left the stage hand-in-hand. I rooted for their love story then the same way I do today.

Matt and I forged a great friendship that day and we haven't looked back. Crazy circumstances brought us together, but I couldn't be happier they did. Few men could walk through the fire of public controversy and come out the other side smiling the way that Matt has. He is a perpetually positive person. He never let the critics kill his spirit.

Over the past year, I have had the pleasure of getting to know the man off-camera. He is a lover of people, a servant of his community, and a man of faith. He is led by his passions, his heart, but most importantly his integrity. He's shown me the core of his character, but even I did not know the foundation that that character was built on. The story ahead opened my eyes to the many trials and tribulations that formed my friend. Matt was never given a lot. Still, he turned the values his mother instilled into a national platform. My respect for him has only increased after reading his remarkable story.

You may have met the man on-screen, but get to know the person, and a journey, that will move your heart and open up your eyes to a life one could only imagine living.

Introduction

No one can prepare you to be the first of your kind. But many will try.

When I received the surprising call offering me the role of the Bachelor, I didn't know my decision would be a groundbreaking one. I hadn't watched the show before. I hadn't even thought much of the show before. If pressed, I would have assumed that a Black man had been chosen as the lead in the past. Hadn't it been on air forever? *Surely* at least one brother had led the franchise. That thought would quickly be proven wrong! I discovered that I would be the first ever Black Bachelor more than a week after accepting the role.

That bit of information heightened the stakes of my choice. It made me question whether I'd made the right decision at all. We were in the midst of a real moment in America. Racial conflict swirled at its highest level in my lifetime. Every day seemed to bring new examples of brutality to contend with. The first announcement of a new, Black Bachelor wouldn't be some great milestone on the march to equality, but it would turn heads. Did I want to inject myself into that crossfire?

My first instinct was to consult my closest confidants. Several friends were also members of Bachelor Nation and had once received similar calls. They shared familiar wisdom: relax, live in the moment, be yourself. As true as their offerings might have been, they weren't very helpful. I turned to Black friends to get their insight. They understood the gravity of the choice in ways that others couldn't, but still didn't have much good advice to offer. In truth, I posed an impossible question. No one's advice could prepare me for the challenge ahead. I had to move ahead on this path alone. During the greatest racial reckoning in a generation, the producers at ABC turned to me to lead one of America's favorite franchises as its first Black star. No one could fully understand the weight of that choice.

As announcement day approached, my emotions crashed in waves. I felt excitement at all the possibilities *The Bachelor* represented—the possibility of love in the short term, and the wide-open, unknowable possibilities of whatever would come after. I felt nervous, wading into a world of flashing lights that I knew nothing about. But soon, above all else, I felt the weight of responsibility. My decisions would be picked apart in ways they hadn't been for Bachelors past. After spending a lifetime in mostly white spaces, I knew what it meant to represent a race to people who didn't know better. But this was a whole different league. I didn't want to mess it up. I also didn't even know what "mess it up" meant. As time went on, the responsibility hardened into a burden.

Fortunately, I had the support of many thousands of people behind me. Messages streamed in by the hundreds when I was announced as the Bachelor. They cheered me on, applauded my choice, and wished me well on my journey. They held high hopes and expectations. They'd be rooting for me, they said. I appreciated the love. Of course, underneath it all, the pressure only increased.

Months later, I watched the premiere of my season of *The Bachelor* from my apartment in New York City. My closest loved ones gathered 'round—I slid in between my roommate, Tyler Cameron, and my mother to watch the episode. I struck a deal with Twitch, the online live-streaming platform, to stream the small viewing party I'd assembled. I interacted in real time with fans during the episode and donated the proceeds to the LeBron James Family Foundation to help fund his I Promise School.

Only three of us gathered in the living room, but I stretched my mind to imagine our audience, the thousands of eyeballs fixed on our every move. I couldn't get too comfortable. I had to keep quiet on the behind-the-scenes tidbits that I might otherwise have spilled. No spoilers allowed. Most of all, I had to keep from reacting, even though I was seeing the episode the same way they all were—for the first time. And, oddly enough, I barely recognized the man on the screen.

I made it through the highs and lows of the episode without blowing my cover. I said goodbye to the viewers before the rose ceremony and cut the TV off. I didn't want to watch myself send a whole group of hopeful women home again. That was brutal.

After watching the premiere, I appreciated, for the first time, just how much of my power I had given away. This had been billed as "my" season, but it wasn't, not really at least. I had a dizzying few months leading up to that moment, but at each step along the way—through preparation and filming—I thought I was in the driver's seat. I didn't remember handing over ownership of my story; but watching the premiere, it was clear that I had. The producers would craft my story now. I had no control over what might follow.

My introduction to America ran five minutes. It spoke little about the people and beliefs I valued most. I understood the constraints of production time. We had a long season ahead of us with plenty left to unpack. But we'd be playing catch-up. First impressions matter, and mine was lacking. Sure, I had assumed that later episodes would present the other sides of me that the premiere left out. But, for the first time, I had doubts about that as well.

So much has changed since my *Bachelor* season began. Some changes were foreseeable. I knew that leading the series would mean sacrificing my anonymity. My friends from Bachelor Nation warned me about the mixed bag that comes with fame. Still, the benefits of the journey always seemed to outweigh the cons of life after.

I'm not so sure today, though. My private life has evaporated away. Regular trips to the grocery store become Page Six headlines. I rarely stroll from my apartment to the subway today without groups of people approaching me along the way. The vast majority of these encounters are fun—fans of the show excited to say hello and then go about their days. I really do love those conversations, brief brushes with other smiling New Yorkers happy to deliver words of encouragement. Online run-ins are, of course, different. If in-person interactions are 98 percent positive, Twitter mentions are the opposite. I try not to pay them much mind. But then there are a few that fall in between the two. Those interactions stay with me long after their end.

A young woman ran up to me in Soho recently—stout, with inky dot eyes and hipster glasses the size of half her face. She reached her hand out for a shake then awkwardly turned it to a hug midway through. In a high-pitched voice, she squeaked, "I love the work you're doing, Matt. You have such a positive influence. Keep going." Though I'd had similar interactions, her words felt oddly reassuring after a long week. I nodded and leaned in when she asked for a selfie, then thanked her for the encouragement. I hugged her again before we parted and then skated off on my way.

She tagged me in a picture later that day. I'd never met the woman before, but I noticed we had a long messaging history. I read the old messages, all from her side. She'd called me everything but a child of God. Snubs, insults, and jabs. I'd made a mistake with my final choice, she said. I never should have been the Bachelor. I was a fraud.

She was the first, but the same thing has happened many times since that day. I'm constantly running into kind, generous people who choose to be harsh online. I admit I think more about them than I should. I've always been such an open person, and I like that about myself. I want to fight my first instinct after meeting them—to become closed-off, skeptical, and jaded. I want to understand the disconnect, for my own satisfaction, if not theirs.

Part of it is the nature of celebrity. Gossip is incurable. Trolls will always troll.

But the issue runs deeper than that too. Bachelor Nation watched me for dozens of hours in 2020. They saw me flirt with gorgeous women. They heard me laugh and cry. They discovered pieces of my backstory. And they believed what the TV told them. After all that, they thought they knew me. But when we meet, the illusion falls away. I'm not the man they thought I was.

A year ago, I was Matt James: a person; a fact; a living, breathing being. Overnight, I became Matt James: a topic of debate, a brand, something to "weigh in" on. I became a proxy for so many of the important conversations Americans were already leaning into—racial justice, interracial relationships, history, and prejudice. I felt proud, having furthered dialogue that was both necessary and long overdue. But the dialogue was weighty as well, and as weeks turned to months, it felt suffocating at times.

But the most difficult part was that, in my conversion from person to prop, key pieces of me were left behind. I am a man of faith, a son, and a brother. I am a mixed kid, an ambitious dreamer, and a tireless striver. I am a Southern boy from North Carolina who reached one of America's largest stages.

These qualities didn't shine through in my season of *The Bachelor* the way I would have liked. They got lost in the fog of drama and distraction. And the misconceptions caused problems of their own—problems bigger than I, or the folks at *The Bachelor*, ever anticipated.

Fortunately, this year was not the first time I faced great challenges. The path from Raleigh to Hollywood was a rocky one, and I learned a few things about overcoming adversity along the way. Those were the lessons I called upon when plunging into the biggest decision of my life, and also when grappling with the unanticipated, yet necessary, controversy my choice created.

This isn't the typical *Bachelor* book. This book is about those lessons, and the sometimes funny, often hard, ways I stumbled into them. This book is about Matt James the man.

The Bachelor told its version of my story. Twitter had its turn too. Now it's time I tell my story for myself and share the lessons I've learned from a lifetime of ignoring unlikely odds.

First Impressions

CHAPTER 1

Be Authentic.
Be Real.

*Defining myself, as opposed to being
defined by others, is one of the most
difficult challenges I face.*
—Carol Moseley Braun

I crashed into controversy on my first episode of *The Bachelor*. I don't think I made it forty-five minutes. The opening parade of women caught me off-guard. It's one thing to be told that you are going to date thirty-two women at once; it is a completely other thing to watch those thirty-two women stream out of limousines in a flourish of sweet scents and sparkles. With each introduction, they one-upped one another.

Why take a limousine to the meet-and-greet when you can take a Bentley?

Why not a throne shouldered by four royal subjects?

Why not a football jersey with my name on it, or lingerie?

Or maybe a sweet memento from home? Hell, why not your vibrator?

Their theatrics only added to their charm. I was so nervous, and sweat dripped off my forehead.

I planned to deliver a grand toast on our first night. I discussed it all with the producers beforehand. I'd kick off the cocktail party with a heartfelt speech about what brought me to the Nemacolin resort, what I looked for in a partner, and all that we had to look forward to in the weeks ahead. This slim part of my first impression would be entirely within my control. The monologue would be my personal introduction to the women and to America.

Thirty-two introductions later, the cocktail party kicked off in the middle of the night. The women mingled together in the living room before I arrived. I darted from the entryway to the bathroom to dab the sweat from my pits and recenter. I inhaled calmness and exhaled angsty air. I mumbled through my opening remarks three times. When I was prepared to join them, I stepped into a room overflowing with beauty. All eyes were on me.

They wiped my mind clean. What was that charming punchline

I was going to deliver? Something about it smelling like roses? I couldn't remember a thing and, as I stood uncomfortably, mouth agape, the awkward silence between us roared loudly.

I raised my glass, asked everyone to bow their heads, and coaxed out the only words I could. Instead of the women, I spoke to God:

"…you said that you work all things for the good of those who love you and are called according to your purpose, Father God, and I feel like that's why I'm here and that's why these women are here, Lord. So, bless this time we have together, Father. In your holy name I pray…"

I opened my eyes feeling already at peace. The words returned to me, and I shared my hopes for the weeks the women and I would spend together.

The prayer sparked the first little fire of the season. Everyone in the media had something to say about that move—was it inappropriate? Overly calculated? Inauthentic? But those who know me, and know the people I'm from, know that my faith is fixed at my core.

My grandparents' household was a deeply Catholic place. It was the Italian in them. Their faith was at least as much cultural as it was spiritual, though. They attended Mass and found family in the other members of their parish. My mother was raised in that faithful community, but by the time she reached adulthood, her faith was withering away fast.

When, in her thirties, she decided to marry my dad, she had

very little faith left at that point in her life, but returned for the parish's blessing for tradition's sake. The priest's mind seemed to have been made up before she even walked through the door. When he told her no, he broke her faith—what little of it was left. Mom had been drifting away from religion for years. She'd seen early sexual scandals in the media and experienced inappropriate behavior up close. The church wasn't the moral vanguard she'd been brought up to respect. But Mom's love for Dad was near all-consuming. Any institution that couldn't respect that wasn't for her.

In a justice of the peace ceremony, they said, "I do," and married life began. Then Dad's antics began (more on those later). The early days of marriage landed hard on Mom. Two years in, and she felt her world was already spinning out of control: she was pregnant with my older brother, John, and increasingly aware that she hadn't married a faithful man. It would still be five more years before she gathered the strength to leave Dad, and another year after that before she got on her feet. So, early in marriage, she was in the eye of the storm, with the end still far off in the distance. She compartmentalized her fears. She was still working full-time, so each day she showed up to her job, tucking the rest of life behind a curtain. But she was an unconvincing actress.

My mother tells the story of Summer, a bubbly, blond-haired co-worker who bounced around their real estate office to a chipper rhythm. Summer exuded joy. She was the opposite of the seriousness Mom felt in her most trying hours. Summer asked Mom to lunch one day, and she accepted out of curiosity—why was this woman so joyful? My mother had maintained her composure through weeks of stresses. When Summer asked her how she was doing, it triggered something inside her. Mom broke down. The two women talked for hours. Summer admitted that she had seen the heaviness that my mother was carrying; she'd been praying for her for weeks. Summer confided the secret to her joy: her relationship with Jesus. As the meal wrapped up, Summer invited Mom to pray with her. Mom bowed her head, closed her eyes, and sobbed as Summer recited the sinner's prayer:

Dear Lord Jesus, I know that I am a sinner, and I ask for Your forgiveness. I believe You died for my sins and rose from the dead. I turn from my sins and invite You to come into my heart and life. I want to trust and follow You as my Lord and Savior. In Your Name. Amen.

When my mother opened her eyes, her faith had been restored. She joined a new church, seeking community in her faith. Mom prayed from that day forward, drawing comfort and peace from His word. Years later, she only remembers Summer as an angel.

Mom pressed faith into John and me just as her parents had done her, but she used the carrot instead of the stick. She drove clear across town each Sunday and Wednesday to deliver us to Raleigh International Church (RIC) for worship services. RIC occupied the large end block of a strip mall off Capital Boulevard, a rough part of town in Raleigh, North Carolina. It sat in a rough neighborhood. Most residents were Black, as was the congregation, but the strip mall catered to the area's growing Latinx population—storeowners hawked Mexican flavors and fare in Spanish all day long. It was a welcome retreat from our white corner of Raleigh.

It wasn't just a happy accident that we ended up in a Black church. We lived in the South, the Bible Belt; we must have passed fifteen churches on our way to RIC. Mom chose RIC for the same reason she enrolled John and me in Amateur Athletic Union basketball (AAU), track, and community center football—if our dad wasn't going to stick around, she'd have to find other Black role models for us. Mom saw the same stereotyped portrayal of Blackness on the TV screens that we did. She wanted to give us more to aspire to. At RIC, she found God-fearing Black men worthy of our admiration.

Inside the church walls, Pastor Olden Thornton commanded our congregation through testimony. He saw the power of God daily, in miracles large and small, and invited others to marvel at the blessings He'd showered upon them. He called for testimony at each service, and unfailingly, every week, a dozen or more souls rose to give witness. These were devoted Christians leading hard lives, yet nobody complained. They focused on the slim margin that kept them from falling further. A man got work after months of unemployment. A woman scraped together enough to fix her flat tire, then the mechanic threw in the transmission for free. A family found a home after months without.

Pastor Thornton noticed the changes swirling in the Southside, and he embraced them. On my first trip to RIC, I joined an all-Black congregation. As the neighborhood demographics shifted, Pastor Thornton held the church doors open for Latinx newcomers. A full-time Spanish translator joined him in leading sermons, and he added new Mexican members to the ranks of deacons and deaconesses. I admired the man's willingness to embrace change. He just wanted to spread the Word. Ministry mattered to him far more than the complexion of his congregation.

The churchgoers changed around us, but one thing remained the same: there was only one white person in that audience. If she ever even noticed, it didn't show. Like Pastor Thornton, Mom was there for worship. She saw everyone else as her siblings in Christ.

I never testified before the congregation, but Mom did. After years of twice-weekly services, she finally took the long walk to the microphone and shared what weighed on her heart. It was a nearly unnoticeable blessing from the week before, but I admired her courage in rising to the head of the room. Others had mixed feelings about this white woman with Black children taking time they thought was theirs. But Mom pressed on. By the time she returned to her seat, the shaking heads had turned to nods and amens.

Mom stopped at KFC on the way home from church each Sunday. John and I gorged on buckets of chicken, smothered mashed potatoes, and honey-covered biscuits. Mom knew what she was doing. That's how she kept us coming back.

Mom taught us the true meaning of faith in more subtle ways as we aged. I witnessed her live her faith between Sundays. Nowhere was it more evident than in her treatment of my father.

No one had more reason to hate my father than Mom. He broke the vows they shared. He neglected his parenting responsibilities. He betrayed her. Yet she never grew bitter. To the contrary, she loved him through it all. She never said a bad word about him to John or me, even though he accused her of poisoning our relationship with him. To this day, he is the only man she ever loved. She stared at his faults and embraced him anyway. And she encouraged us to do the same. When I was young, I saw her tendency to forgive as a sign of weakness. I grew frustrated, wishing she'd boil in pain, anger, and disappointment the way I often did.

I had to mature to see how wrong I was. Her forgiveness was her strength. It was her wisdom. And her unshakable faith enabled it in her. Faith taught her we were all flawed, all works in progress, and yet worthy of love nonetheless. Each day, I try to come closer to embracing that spirit, which she embodied so effortlessly. At the beginning of the pandemic, my former teammates at Wake Forest and I started a men's

> Faith taught her we were all flawed, all works in progress, and yet worthy of love nonetheless.

Bible study group that grew week by week and still continues to meet today.

I grew in my faith throughout my childhood, following Mom's example. I learned to lean on it in times of adversity, and it gave me strength. Later, as I matured, and the challenges did too, faith brought me peace in times of torment. On the opening night of *The Bachelor*, faced with a room full of beautiful strangers and on the precipice of the most daunting adventure of my life, *of course* I leaned on my faith. It runs through me. I needed the peace it provides.

Sadly, the prayer was not the only controversy I stirred in my first hour of national television.

Early in the evening, before any of the women arrived, the nerves had already struck. Moments before I was set to welcome them from the front steps of the resort, I pulled the show's host to the side to talk. We entered a room to the side, and I unloaded the burden that had kept my chest tight.

In the months leading up to that moment, people had emerged from the woodwork to offer their best dating advice. Internet trolls and armchair psychologists shared their opinions on my "type." I dismissed most of what I heard. But the comment that came most frequently, I took seriously: "You know you have to pick a Black girl, right?"

This pressure would be uniquely mine, different from all the white Bachelors who preceded me. Mass media had long diminished the beauty of Black women and the prevalence of healthy, loving, Black relationships. Nowhere was this more evident than in *The Bachelor* itself, where I was the first Black man to lead the series after two decades on air. I was in a privileged position. I could make a declaration on the worthiness of Black love on one of America's grandest stages. The cliché of the successful Black man settling with a white partner is well understood; there would be symbolic value in my turning away from others to find love among my own people. Others were reasonable to expect things of me. My position came with responsibility. It weighed on me in part because I knew I might disappoint all the people who had once cheered me on.

Soon, I would meet more than two dozen women who had traveled to Nemacolin to join our season. Many would be non-Black. I couldn't just write those others off when they'd taken such a leap of faith in hope of finding love. Nor would I want to. My personal history wouldn't let me push them aside. I was born to a white woman. A white woman nurtured me all my life and is my best friend today. How could I preemptively reject all white women when my own mother is one?

I voiced my turmoil to the host. I poured my heart out for more than an hour, stressing over the impossible choice before me—an openness to love in all its many forms on one side and a duty to my people on the other. It felt impossible to please everyone.

Our side conversation spanned a few minutes of TV time when

it aired. It lacked the nuance I tried to capture. I didn't recognize it as the same heartfelt interaction I'd had. Twitter lifted sound bites and reframed them further. They made it sound as though I had made my mind up on night one: I wouldn't choose a Black woman—literally the opposite of the point I tried to make. Accusations that I was an Uncle Tom followed, and that pained me.

The expectations felt uncomfortable, but not unfamiliar. As a biracial boy raised in the South, racial conflict always existed inside me as much as around me. Why should this new journey be any different?

I struggled to form relationships with other Black kids when I was young. For one, there weren't any. Our section of Raleigh was white, white, white. In all my years of lower school, I can remember only ever having one Black classmate—Tommy—who became a close friend, but two is a few short of a crew.

When I did meet other Black kids at basketball or Sunday school, everything was all good...until pickup time arrived. My stomach tightened when I heard my mom's voice and turned to see her strolling up the pavement.

Inevitably, someone hollered out, "*THAT'S* your mom?"

Other voices followed. They could be punishing—Oreo, white boy, wigger—anything other than what I was.

I understand the confusion—and the punchlines that followed it—in hindsight. We were all kids trying to make sense of the world, and they'd learned that mom plus dad equals son. I appear fully Black. I don't have taupe skin, hazel eyes, or bouncing curls. Dad's Nigerian genes were strong.

My white half meant something different at school, a whole world reserved for whiteness. I grew close to my white classmates, but they too spoke about my race. Going to friends' houses, I heard them introduce me, "Mom, Dad, this is my friend Matt," always closely followed by "he's half white." They saw a part of themselves in me, and it made me worthy. I saw the difference in how they treated Tommy. Tommy didn't get the privilege of whitening that I enjoyed.

During my early teens, the confusion moved beyond my family tree and on to cultural cues. Blackness came with expectations then. All kids—white and Black alike—had fully formed understandings of Blackness and what it meant. I stretched to fit into these new molds but rarely did. Growing up around all white people, in a house led by a white woman, I'd already missed too much. I still remember the earliest of those awkward initial attempts to grow into my Blackness.

I was in middle school and had traveled to Disney World for nationals with my AAU basketball team, a collection of basketball players across the state of North Carolina who were predominantly Black with the exception of one white player. The whole team plus chaperones packed into a hotel room one evening to bond over large pizzas and Call of Duty. I rocked an afro like it was a nappy halo then. In the middle of the action, my teammate's mom tapped me on the shoulder, "Okay, Matt, your turn to get braided." I followed her to the sofa, bitter to drop the game controller but excited to get my cornrows back. I sat between her legs with my back to her, craning to keep a good view of the TV. She plunged her fingers into my knotted web. And that's when she said it:

"Damn, baby, your hair is dry."

The action stopped. The beady eyes and ears gathered around the room perked up. Some shot their glances over to me, hushed down, and waited. I understood the stakes—one wrong move here, and I'd be the butt of a joke for the whole ride home from Florida.

"No, ma'am. My hair is not dry. I wash it every day," I said.

The room remained silent for a moment, and then:

"You do what?"

Shit! Laughter erupted. Oh, God. Here we go...

"Matt has that nappy 'fro."

"Matt got the Nigerian Kunta Kinte braids."

"I knew somethin' wasn't right with that head!"

I'm not sure it's possible for a Black man to blush, but I swear, that afternoon, my face turned ruby red.

Grooming was an issue from that day forward. First, dry hair, then ashy elbows, then razor bumps. It would be years before I learned how to shave my Black beard properly. Other issues arose too—clothes, music, and dance. Black homes handed these lessons down to the young ones. Mom did her best to teach two Black boys their culture in our home, but she could only do so much.

When it came to dating, Mom was as easygoing as they come. She wanted me to be happy and to find a girl who cared for me completely. Her babies, the joys of her life, were products of an interracial marriage. She didn't have an opinion on race one way or the other.

My early relationships, if that's what you call week-long middle school romances, were all with white girls. That wasn't so much a choice as it was the natural outcome of circumstance. I only dated white girls because I only knew white girls. Again, North Raleigh equals white.

Because our part of town was so white, I didn't even know then that dating white girls *could* be problematic. The small handful of other Black guys at my school dated white girls also—they didn't know anyone else either. The same was true for the couple Black girls at my school. We couldn't give one another grief because we were all dealing with the same constrained choices. I wanted to explore relationships with people who looked like me but found few places to turn where I saw *us*.

Age presented opportunity. The dating pool opened as life progressed. I moved out of Raleigh and dated Black women in later years, including in my time leading up to joining *The Bachelor*. I felt warmth seeing a piece of myself reflected in them. Each was a phenomenal person. Blackness informed their characters in brilliant ways, but it didn't determine them. I was attracted to the individuals they were.

I arrived at my *Bachelor* debut with decades of experience navigating the complicated expectations of Blackness. But the show brought about a new level of scrutiny. The criticism infuriated me. My Blackness hadn't been openly challenged in years. I wanted to scream, "Who are you calling a...?!?" at every rogue DM that hit my in-box. But firing back at trolls is never a good move; to do so would just encourage the back-and-forth. Instead, I returned to the tools I learned in childhood.

As I matured, the only way I could stay positive was by embracing all sides of myself equally; to deny any single part would be too painful. Yes, I am Black, proudly and unapologetically so. I am white also, Italian to be exact, and I'm proud of that too. And when picking a partner, the most intimate choice there is, I had to honor both sides of myself and follow where my heart led.

I lump the two "Day One" controversies together because they happened simultaneously, but also because they were the same type. America processing my conflicting identities—Christian in an increasingly secular world; Black *and* white. My reaction to both was the same as well. I remembered who I was and pressed on. I pledged to be my most authentic self on that show, just as I strive to be in life. I center my understanding of myself on the qualities and principles I possess. Third parties don't determine the man I am.

> Third parties
> don't determine
> the man I am.

There are so many ways in which our identities can conflict today. Nationalities or religions that diverge based on genders, worldviews, or races—there are unlimited opportunities for us to get mixed up in ourselves. The only thing to do with that conflict is to rise above it, to state firmly that you are one whole person and are living proof that we humans can be many things at once. That is the only way to remain confident in a world that would rather see you pick a side.

If I knew this lesson intellectually for my first twenty-nine years of life, accepting the role of the first Black Bachelor put it to the test. Fortunately, I had a lot of life to call upon, years of experiencing betweenness. The people behind those experiences shaped me more than they even realize.

CHAPTER 2

Roots Run Deep

*A man without knowledge of himself and
his heritage is like a tree without roots.*
—Dick Gregory

I skated through the neighborhood, blissfully unaware, when the world shook. The epicenter of the quake was somewhere off in the middle of the country. But it wouldn't be long before the aftershocks reached Florida. The next morning, I lay in bed scrolling Twitter, when I first saw the video and felt the earth shift beneath me.

It showed a man dead in the street. Above him kneeled a police officer, grinding him deeper into gravel. The man looked like me in the general sense that all Black men could just as easily be me and me them. But he *really* looked like my father in an inescapably specific sense. More stretched out and muscular, but the same dark skin and broad nose. Or maybe not. I couldn't see his face clearly while it was pancaked to the pavement.

The man didn't put up much of a fight. He was cuffed already by the time I saw him. He pleaded and squirmed. The man wheezed, and the officer kneeled. The man begged for relief, and the officer kneeled. The man hacked up his final, strained breaths before lying motionless. And still, the officer kneeled. Minutes later, medics arrived to unceremoniously lift the lifeless body onto a gurney and wheel it away.

This cell phone video, attached to a stranger's tweet, told me everything and nothing at once. I needed context. Surely, I didn't really just watch the last moments of a man's life, did I? Couldn't have. My corner of the Twittersphere was just as silly and unbothered as ever. This must be a deep fake or a troll's doing. He was a wanted criminal, threatening violence. Or had we all become so desensitized to Black death that even this violent video couldn't get a rise out of folks?

All my guesses were wrong. I wasn't missing anything. I was just early.

The video ricocheted around the world twice and landed in my roommate's bedroom within the hour. Tyler stormed into my room in a huff, holding up his phone as evidence: "Have you seen this?" I nodded without looking at the screen. The stunned look on his face reflected how I felt inside. I checked back in to Twitter. The storm had started.

Information trickled in. The city had a name: Minneapolis. The man did too: George Floyd. His final words, "I can't breathe," were eerily identical to Eric Garner's years earlier, and already users chanted them around the web. The officer didn't have a name yet, but he would soon enough.

I lived in Jupiter, Florida, at the time—a three-week stay that had extended to months. I was crashing at Tyler Cameron's house, my closest friend and, under normal circumstances, my roommate in New York. But these weren't normal circumstances. The world had just shut down for the coronavirus pandemic, and I escaped to the sunshine of South Florida to ride out the worst of it. So had ten others; the Cameron household swelled with escapees from every corner of the country, resolved that, if we must endure a pandemic, we should do it together.

I was thankful to have so many others nearby—there are worse ways to ride out a pandemic than alongside your closest friends. But they were all white, and though that hadn't mattered as recently as one day ago, after watching the video of George Floyd's murder, it was unavoidable. I felt very isolated in our crowded home.

Tyler rescued me from turning the images over in my mind for too long. Perhaps he couldn't feel Floyd's death as viscerally as I had, but he came close. Tyler was raised in a home that welcomed people of all stripes. Sports brought him closer to Black people and at a younger age than even I could claim. His anguish reflected my anguish, and he wasn't afraid to dive into the difficult conversations that had to follow.

Tyler listened more than he spoke. Soon, he was asking me my opinions on the event, its roots, and its broader implications. He wasn't the only one. Months earlier, I'd been announced as a contestant on *The Bachelorette*. Filming stalled due to the pandemic, but the announcement itself, combined with my closeness to Tyler, who had grown a large platform of his own, placed more eyes on me than ever before. I was expected to have an opinion and to share it. But other than the grief that I shared with so many others, I didn't have much to say. For the first time, it struck me—I didn't know my history any better than my white friends did. How could I? We'd lived nearly identical lives.

With the downtime the pandemic created, I began my self-education. I reached out to the Black men I respected, friends I'd made in adulthood whom I knew had the knowledge. They shared their author recommendations, names I'd known but only indirectly—Du Bois, Coates, and Baldwin. Lists floated around social media of required reading for those in need of an awakening. I read more, and each time I finished, I passed the book off to Tyler, who did the same.

If context was what I wanted, I got it from books, not Twitter.

I saw the lines now from slave catchers to police forces. From red-lining to the Black neighborhoods police patrolled. Tyler and I reached identical realizations simultaneously. What was the point of having a platform if not to advocate for justice?

I posted the same Black square that I saw plastered across Instagram feeds and attached the Bible verse that spoke to me in that moment, Galatians 5:22–23: "But the fruit of the Spirit is love, joy, peace, forbearance, kindness, goodness, faithfulness, gentleness and self-control. Against such things there is no law." I acknowledged, like many, that the move would be insufficient. But those words spoke a message of rightness, resilience, and resolve to me in a moment when I needed to hear it. I hoped the message could land on others who needed the same.

Protests streamed through Jupiter just as they did in cities across America. Tyler and I joined the marches, carrying signs emblazoned with those haunting last words, "I can't breathe." Community leaders schooled us on the local histories that had led to division

> "But the fruit of the Spirit is love, joy, peace, forbearance, kindness, goodness, faithfulness, gentleness and self-control. Against such things there is no law."
> —Galatians 5:22–23
>
> …Those words spoke a message of rightness, resilience, and resolve to me in a moment when I needed to hear it.

across Florida. They told us about national organizations combating injustice, fighting the good fight. I used my platform to amplify their important efforts.

I was tuned in to the national conversation now, and I steamed with frustration at the dialogue I heard. Well-intentioned folks spoke about the issues that began with Trayvon Martin. A decade of Black death. But I looked at the video of George Floyd and saw so much more. I saw the legacy of lynching. The long history of police violence. The institutional forces that thrust Floyd and his murderer into collision on an underfunded street corner.

The public conversation ignored how history had delivered us to this pivotal moment. The omission taught me a lesson that I took to heart. A true story must start at the beginning. And the beginning must stretch further into the past than we imagine. You must dig deep to pull up roots. And the root explains the fruit.

Floyd's fate was fresh in my mind when I sat down to begin writing this book. I still felt the anguish. But I also considered it in the context of the stories we tell ourselves. For obvious reasons, I thought a lot about the importance of a story then. A truth that is bound up in a single moment isn't as true. I realized that, to tell my story truthfully, I must go back to the beginning.

My story begins at the turn of the century with four Italians on two steamboats to the new world. My great-grandparents struck out from the old country with empty pockets and hearts full of hope. Their children, John Cuculo and Eve Cortese, met as twenty-somethings on a summer evening in the backroom of a Providence social club. They married soon after and moved together when John was admitted to a PhD program in chemical engineering at Duke University.

The Cuculo couple built a lovely life for themselves. John finished his PhD, and the two started a family—three daughters made their family complete. John spent a decade in industry before returning to academia, becoming a professor at North Carolina State. The girls spent their teenage years in a professor's house. Every Thursday, students arrived in droves for Eve's food and John's drink. Students crossed the globe to come to NC State's chemical engineering program, so the Cuculo household resembled a model UN conference. The girls enjoyed a loving life—two happy parents, annual vacations, and a white picket fence to protect it all.

The eldest Cuculo daughter was a goody-goody and the youngest kept to herself, but Patty, the middle one, inherited her mother's headstrong demeanor. She butted heads with her father early and often in childhood. But, perhaps because of their differences, the two were inseparable. Patty was close with her mother too; she learned to cook the large spaghetti dinners that her mother and her mother's mother before her once whipped up. Life for them then was an episode of *The Brady Bunch*.

She didn't know it then, but childhood would be a high point for Patty, before the valley of young adulthood. She married young, as a college student, and spent her twenties in a loveless marriage that ended in disappointment. She tried and failed many times to bear children, eventually assuming she couldn't. Then she split from her first husband and moved back to her hometown.

Nearly thirty-five years old now, Patty hit a stride in her new life. She returned to Raleigh. She worked a job with American Airlines registering the time cards for Raleigh-Durham airport's fleet service clerks, the neon-vested men who motion planes into parking spots. She reported to the underground belly of the airport and took time cards from plane wavers. And then one of them stole her heart.

Emmanuel James, Manny, landed in Raleigh still fresh from a voyage across the world. He struck out from his home, Nigeria, in search of prosperity. He came to Raleigh for the American Airlines job and soon learned the macarena of plane waving. On lunch breaks and after long days, he sauntered to Patty's desk and flirted in accented English. He always had something clever to say. He never failed to notice a new haircut or fresh manicure. Patty was drawn in to Manny immediately—his deep-set eyes and unblemished skin; his high cheekbones and the broad smile he draped between them. He was eleven years her junior, but she didn't mind the age gap. He was hilarious, charming, and ambitious.

They fell into a relationship that John, Patty's father, was uncomfortable with. He tried more than once to talk Patty out of it. He never liked Manny. He warned his daughter not to get involved with the strange man with a stranger accent. She never had to wonder why: "I don't want you dating a Black man. You're asking for a more difficult life than you need."

These arguments were no different than the ones they had had in that same house twenty years before. The longer they had it out, the further they receded into their own corners. The fights produced tears, and resentment, and division, but little else, so he soon dropped it. John's work took him out of the country for months on end, and Eve typically followed for his trips away. One year into Patty's relationship, with a trip soon approaching, John asked her to house-sit. He made it clear that an unmarried couple wouldn't live under his roof. Fortunately, Patty had a simple solution. Patty and Manny were married before a justice of the peace. They honeymooned in John and Eve's home.

Patty enjoyed a time of bliss. Manny remained charismatic and kept her laughing through their first year together. Then they received their first blessing.

When, six months into her new marriage, Patty found out she was pregnant, she sprung a leak and cried tears of joy until she had nothing left. She birthed a baby boy. After years of believing she was infertile, the new life in her hands seemed like a mirage. She named the boy John after her father, the wise professor.

Two years later, she received what must have been the greatest blessing to ever arrive in her life. Another baby boy. This one she named Matthew. And then I got to rename everyone else. John Sr. became Grandpa; Eve, Grandma; Patty, Mom; Manny, Dad; and John Jr., my big brother.

Dad continued to work at American Airlines, but Mom left; she had other work to tend to now. Dad's job provided just enough for Mom to stay home and care for the two of us. She embraced the joys and challenges of new motherhood.

Grandpa's attitude worsened when John and I arrived. Mom had brought two mixed kids into the world, and Grandpa couldn't face it. Mom and Grandpa's relationship cooled further.

The arrivals of John and me were high points in a marriage that otherwise began to sour. The honeymoon phase ended with suspicion. Dad frequently traveled around the country for free on the airline's dime. He visited his brother in New York. Or his brother met him in cities dotting the West—Los Angeles, San Francisco, and Las Vegas. Sometimes he returned a day late. Sometimes he returned smelling like sweet roses. Sometimes Mom wondered whether he'd return at all. All the while, Mom cared for the toddlers at home.

Her suspicion deepened when the calls started. Every few months, a different woman called to expose the relationship she kept up with Dad. Some were in love. Most reassured Mom that he loved her and would never leave. Their words did little to console her.

When Mom confronted Dad, he denied everything. These were crazy women acting the way that crazy women act. What's her name? He'd never even met her before. Stop being ridiculous and put a smile on. Today, we call it gaslighting.

It wasn't just their relationship that suffered; Dad's work life soon did too. In the break room one afternoon, Dad grew impatient waiting for his turn at the microwave. His co-worker just wouldn't step away. Polite asks turned to stern warnings, which turned to shouts. I've heard conflicting accounts of what happened next, but a few facts are clear. Dad got into a fight. Food was thrown. Fists, also, were thrown. The co-worker's ankle was broken. Dad was fired the next day. The boss told him that his hands were tied. Even the worker's union couldn't protect Dad after such a blatant violation.

With that, Dad lost the one source of real pride in his life. It initiated a downward spiral for him. The infidelity worsened. With it, so did his and Mom's relationship. He delivered more denials, and she continued to ignore the red flags. But the phone calls grew more frequent and the trips longer.

Finally, Mom received undeniable proof that Dad had been unfaithful. That's how she describes it—"undeniable." I've never asked what that proof was, but it was enough to shake her into action. She thought about her two young boys and the household she'd raise us in. She wanted us to know the peace and love that had overwhelmed the house she grew up in. She wanted us to look up to our father from a far enough distance to obscure his many flaws.

Mom phoned Grandpa and told him that things had become unbearable. He'd witnessed the decline in their relationship over the years. He'd always expected to receive this call; in fact, it took longer than he'd anticipated. He spoke over Mom's sobs, telling her that she could come back home. It was the answer she needed to hear, yet she sobbed harder when accepting.

Dad left for another of his weekend trips, and Mom made her move. She rented a storage unit and a moving truck and packed up her half of the house. The last pieces of cargo were the most precious—she fastened John and me into our car seats and drove us to our temporary home. She never stopped loving my father, but she never turned back either. I was barely two years old when she left. She and Dad never reunited, and I would never again share a home with them both.

Sometimes I think about what Grandpa must have felt when Mom finally, after years of troubles, raised her hand and asked for help. Surely, he was concerned for her; he'd watched her endure pain long enough. She was his daughter, after all. But I've always wondered whether, beneath the empathy, an indignant "I told you so" simmered. It might have taken longer than he anticipated, but time had proven him right. Manny was wrong for her after all.

If he felt vindicated, he kept it to himself. His child needed him, and he'd be there for her, but he wasn't going to be overwhelmingly warm about it. Grandpa told Mom that she could come home, and she could bring us, her new Black babies. But he'd only allow her to stay seven months. After that, she'd have to find somewhere else to go.

All in a weekend, Mom moved us into her childhood home. I think about how difficult that must have been for her; how much pride she must have had to swallow to step so far into the past.

Mom had been a stay-at-home mom for a few years when American Airlines fired Dad. With Mom out of the workforce and Dad looking for a job, she asked him to apply for welfare. At forty-two years old, she lived with her parents; she was on Medicaid for the first time in her life and could only afford to feed John and me because of food stamps. She felt she'd reached rock bottom.

Soon as we moved to my grandparents' home, Mom began digging us out of the hole we'd fallen into. She applied for jobs. She was told no. She applied for more jobs. All the while, she balanced the pressures of a ticking clock and two open mouths to feed. She tried to keep us out of her parents' way.

Mom received a job offer on the first day of the seventh month. A nearby apartment building needed a new leasing officer, and she jumped at it. Best of all, the job came with a discounted rate on a small, two-bedroom unit. We had a new space to call home. Mom moved the three of us out the following week. She was able to let go of welfare soon after.

Our first apartment in Raleigh was just like the many that

would follow it. Small, one bedroom for Mom and one for John and me to share. A whisper in one room echoed as a shout in the others. But it was ours, and we enjoyed the private space that kept us close.

With this new foundation, Mom went about constructing our childhoods. She felt guilty placing us in day care after years of full-time motherhood, so she turned every spare moment away from work into quality time. Mom didn't want John and me to have a second of downtime—bored boys become troublemakers. She enrolled us in every activity she could find. She learned the ropes of scholarship applications and got us free memberships to the YMCA. From the age of three or four, we took dribbling classes at the local rec center and learned running form on nearby Shaw University's track. As we aged, those early lessons blossomed into AAU basketball tournaments and citywide track meets. Our neighborhood was all white, but sports brought us together with Black kids from across Raleigh. Mom wanted us to see folks who looked like us. She stood against John or me playing football, until the local Pop Warner coach showed up on our doorstep with a recruitment pitch. After some convincing on his, John's, and my part, she relented. In second grade, my football career began.

Our small but mighty family unit formed a tight bond. It was just us three everywhere we went. We had to care for one another. As John and I grew into little men, we became increasingly protective of Mom and each other. Despite our carefree childhoods, we sensed our vulnerability. When your family is only three people, a strong breeze can bring the whole house tumbling down. We watched each other's backs and grew guarded for protection.

After years of struggling—bouncing between jobs and trying hard as she might to keep us in the same apartment we'd grown to love—Mom found a job that checked all her boxes. She sold home security systems. Her pay was 100 percent commission, and what she sacrificed in security, she made up for in flexibility. The new role allowed her to work when she wanted. If she hit her numbers, no one would come looking for her.

Mom worked odd hours and filled the extra time with her other job: motherhood. She became a fixture in the cheering section at our games. She cooked dinner at least once per week, ensuring we ate as a family.

I think back on my lower school years and marvel at my mother's strength. In a handful of years, she went from heartbreak and food stamps to an independent career providing for John and me. At every crucial intersection, she chose the path of bravery. Leaving my father, getting off food stamps, quitting jobs to spend time with us—none of those could have been easy decisions. She sacrificed endlessly for John's and my sake. We weren't rich, but we always had enough. And because our whole world only extended to the apartment complex borders, we didn't know what we were missing. She shielded us from just how difficult her journey was. She protected our childhood innocence with everything she had.

Our shared struggle drew us close. But unintentionally, so did Grandpa. Even after Mom got on her feet and put the worst of her years with Dad behind her, Grandpa continued to distrust and despise the man. I never saw them in a room together; he wouldn't allow it. And on the rare occasions that Dad's name came up in Grandpa's company, he tensed up involuntarily, like the name had singed a nerve.

Grandpa acted like Dad's genes had poisoned John and me too. Whatever was worth despising in Dad was also in us. Grandpa never told us how he felt, but we sensed it all the same. He greeted us with a frosty chill, never the warm embrace he offered others. He barely spoke during our afternoons together. He wasn't at all a loving father figure like the friendly old folks we saw on TV.

Grandpa spent all his love on his other grandkids. Both of my mother's sisters had children before John and I were born. They gave us four cousins. Four white cousins. One pair lived in Raleigh, a few miles away, and the other two lived in Virginia. I loved my older cousins then just as I do now, but I noticed from a young age how they were treated differently.

When we reached elementary school, we spent some afternoons in our grandparents' kitchen, quietly scribbling away at our homework when work kept Mom away late. John had a learning disability that made math difficult to grasp. He turned to Grandpa for help when multiplication and division seemed like impassable brick walls. Mind you, Grandpa held a PhD in chemical engineering. He had been a professor to countless young engineers at the highest levels. Teaching fourth grade math would have been a light lift, to say the least. Still he refused. Instead, he scolded John for his weak grades. Eventually, John stopped asking for help. He'd rather fall behind in class than deal with Grandpa's grief.

It was tradition in our family to return to the grandparents' house each year for Christmas celebrations. Both of Mom's sisters came with their families and filled the house with high spirits and gratitude. We gathered 'round in Grandpa's den and said a prayer. Our cousins salivated over the bright colored wrapping all through the blessing, but John and I knew not to expect much. The big boxes were for the white cousins. Our gift was some small throw-away trinket stuffed in the back. I don't mean to sound ungrateful; we appreciated anything we received. But our gifts were so insignificant compared to the human-sized packages our cousins conquered that one had to wonder why. It was another not-so-subtle reminder of what Grandpa thought of his darker grandchildren.

Still, it wasn't the most obvious example. Grandpa never told us he loved us. That bothered me more than any of the other petty acts. If six different "I love yous" rang out from six different grandchildren, only four were returned. This was a brightly colored billboard compared to the other microaggressions he dealt us throughout our childhoods. Our unanswered "I love yous" told us all that we needed to know. We stopped saying it altogether.

When John and I hit our teenage years, we continued to go to our grandparents' place from time to time, though less frequently, despite feeling unwelcome. We sidestepped the tension once we arrived. We played Nintendo in silence in the back bedroom while Mom visited. If he entered a room, we exited. It was that simple.

We grew more indignant with age. In high school, if we needed a couch to crash on between practices, or just wanted to get out of the house, we showed up unannounced and made ourselves at home. We knew Grandpa didn't want us there, but we were his daughter's children. What was he going to do about it?

We had just left our grandparents' house one day and were on our way back to the apartment when we got a call from Mom. Grandpa had fallen. As we spoke, he was on the ground and couldn't get to his feet. His calls for help had gone unanswered. He finally reached Mom by wriggling around to his side and eking the flip phone out of his back pocket. He didn't think he was seriously hurt, but who knew? Mom's voice shook with concern. She couldn't leave work, and Grandma was miles away. Would we turn around and get him on his feet?

John erupted in laughter. I joined him. Hell no, we wouldn't. This wasn't even a close call. How far would Grandpa go to help either of us? Would he buy duplicates of the big box gifts he wrapped for his other grandkids? Would he share a slice of the knowledge floating around his big brain? Would he speak three simple words to kids who needed to hear them? No, no, no. There you have it. We had our answer.

Mom pleaded with us. Her voice strained further, cutting and returning in unsteady rhythm like Morse code. I began to waver. John held firm. The worry in Mom's voice climbed a few octaves. I quieted, not wanting to give in before John, yet increasingly affected by Mom's stress. For ten minutes, John kept Mom on speaker and the car on track toward home. I locked my jaw shut, trying to appear as resolved as he was. Mom was in tears now. All at once, John let out a groan and swerved the car across traffic and in the opposite direction. He pointed us toward Grandpa's house. I released a silent sigh. Mom repeated *thank you* over and over.

I called out Grandpa's name when we arrived and got a grumpy groan in response. John and I followed it to the kitchen. There lay our patriarch, twisted on the tile floor. A flurry of envelopes and an overturned chair were scattered around him. He turned to us. "Finally! Boys, come get me up." John and I froze. We stared down at him, breathing in his helplessness. I opened my mouth to speak, then thought better of it. "What are you waiting for? Come…" His eyes met ours, and he quieted. No one said a word for a long while. The silence thickened the air and filled the space. Then, as though the debaters in his brain had settled their argument, John stepped forward, squatted, and hooked Grandpa's right arm with his own. I righted the overturned chair, and John dropped Grandpa into it. Back on solid ground, Grandpa heaved a breathy "thank you, boys." We didn't respond. More moments passed.

"Why don't you love us, Grandpa?" The question snuck up on me and spilled out of my mouth before I could catch it. Grandpa jumped; he dropped his head, closed his eyes, and inhaled. Silence. When he looked up again, water had gathered in the corners of his eyes. I was at a loss as to what to call the emotion I saw on his face that day. A mixture of confusion, shame, and pain stuck in the empty cavity where pride once sat. Whatever this emotion was, I'd never seen it on my grandfather before.

Grandpa stopped and started many times before answering. He'd lost his eloquence. He stammered through what followed, but we pieced together the message. He hated our father for how he'd treated our mother. Even today, he felt protective of her. He let it impact how he thought of us. Grandpa admitted his emotions ran deeper than that, though. He grew up in a different time. A different world. He was "old-fashioned." "Traditional." "Narrow-minded." A long list of words that stopped short of racist. But he did love us. He loved us as much as any one of his grandchildren. I think he thought he meant it.

Our conversation ended with a long hug. He wasn't injured and said he'd be fine to continue about his day. He squeezed us tight before sending us on our way.

Our relationship improved from that day. He stopped his passive hostility. I never again saw him as vulnerable and empathetic as he was on the kitchen floor. We never got super close, but we learned to live with one another in harmony. He told me the war stories from his early career. We shared occasional laughs and warm words. Compared to where we started, that felt like a gift.

Grandpa fell ill a few years after we picked him up off the floor. A recent hip replacement had caused an infection. The infection caused sepsis—his body released chemicals to kill the bacteria, but they killed him instead. I visited him in hospice in his final hour. He was a shell of himself, unable to speak. I held his frail hand. I was in twelfth grade when he died. He was eighty-five years old.

The ceremony we held days later felt like the funeral of a stranger. Family members stood to speak about a man who sounded unfamiliar. John didn't shed a tear. I did, though. I mourned what we lost, but also what we never really had.

Grandpa, Grandma, Mom, Dad. This is my history. These are the people I come from. Their stories were written before I was born, but their decisions laid the groundwork for everything that followed. Their strengths became my example. Their flaws became my baggage. No telling of my story could be complete without the context their lives provide.

George Floyd's murder showed America the depths of our injustice. White and Black Americans alike learned something about the darkness our country harbors today. Like many, I'm still grappling with how best to confront that hate without losing hope. But the event taught me another lesson: the importance of historical trauma. Past scars have a way of resurfacing if unresolved. Just as Floyd's end must be understood in the context of a brutal American history, everything of my story that follows can only be understood in the context of my family's history. How else can I account for the difficult lows and totally unexpected highs of my life?

Few people, I have found, are willing to confront their own flawed histories honestly. Avoidance is easier. Individuals operate in the same way that our nation does. When faced with trauma, adversity, or roadblocks of unprecedented magnitude, many people stare within: What did I do to get here? What can I do to get out?

Still others look *around*: Which of my circumstances are to blame? Who failed?

> Past scars have a way of resurfacing if unresolved.

Too few people look back. We should, though. Discontent, like success, has deeper roots than we imagine.

From his kitchen floor, Grandpa taught me that difficult histories can be overcome. He showed me that it is possible for a damaged relationship to mend, and that when it does, both parties heal. We never became the best of friends, but we learned how to live alongside each other with grace and care. And on the day that we laid him to rest, I knew that the man held love in his heart for me.

Most importantly, Grandpa taught me that grace has an expiration date. The best time to heal old wounds is today. I shudder thinking about the regrets I'd have had if my grandfather passed away without us confronting our issues. Don't wait until later to face your pain; later might never come.

CHAPTER 3

Character of a Man

*It isn't where you come from; it's where
you're going that counts.*
—Ella Fitzgerald

I know precious few facts about my father, Manny James. I know
he was born and raised in Lagos, Nigeria. I don't know the stories
of his childhood; he wasn't around enough during mine for me to
learn them. I know his father was a riot policeman. I know his cop
father was gunned down in the streets of Lagos and died young. I
know that shaped the man my father became, though I don't know
exactly how.

Dad chased opportunity to America at nineteen years old. He

didn't know a soul on the continent except for his big brother, but that was enough. He flew from Nigeria to New York and shacked up with his brother in the Bronx. The job with American Airlines led him to Raleigh soon after, and to my mother soon after that.

I don't remember a time when my parents were ever together. I was a newborn when they separated, and Dad moved off to Durham. Anything before that, the days they spent together, the romance they once shared, is all secondhand knowledge.

My memory of Dad picks up in a used car lot. *His* used car lot. John and I spent sporadic weekends with him in the early elementary years. He picked us up after school on Friday or early Saturday morning and drove us out to the junkyard he made his kingdom.

After losing the job at American Airlines, Dad became a used car salesman. He traveled to auctions across the state to purchase lemons that he fixed up—barely—and resold for profit. The lot claimed a few acres of Durham dirt that butted up against a trailer park. At one end of the property, elevated on a grassy knoll, sat a trailer; Dad dropped it on the property to serve as the car lot office.

Dad moved from Raleigh to be near his new lot and bought another double-wide trailer to live in. His new home sat on cinder blocks at the end of a spindly, uneven dirt road. The trailer looked more like a prefab building than a motor home; there weren't any wheels on the bottom or porthole windows to peer from. It was khaki-colored with forest-green shutters. His space was loosely controlled chaos—last night's pizza, dirty dishes, a few Nigerian trinkets. The sour scent of stale weed wafted through the whole home.

Time with Dad wasn't really time *with* Dad. It was barely even time in Dad's presence. He worked, and John and I knew to steer clear while he was engaged with customers. We found ways to keep ourselves busy instead.

Dad kept a rusty, off-brand tractor on the property. The rickety contraption lurched to stops and starts and hacked up black smoke in between. John and I treated it like a Ferrari. Each time we pulled onto the lot, we threw open the car doors and raced to the tractor's driver's seat. Loser had to spend the day in the back seat. I always lost.

John zoomed us around the car lot at twelve miles per hour. I tumbled off for secret missions, then sprinted to hop back on. He let out screeches and roars each time he rounded a row of cars. John took a few of those corners too tight. He rammed the tractor into the merchandise. We got off with a warning the first time and a spanking the second. On the third, it was bye-bye, tractor privileges.

Dad was a massive DMX fan. He liked X's music, but he loved his movies. In fact, he loved all the hood classics from that era. *Cradle 2 the Grave, Paid in Full, Romeo Must Die.* Anything where hip-hop, violence, and sex collided on the big screen.

Mom never let us watch the movies of the day, but at Dad's, we had free rein. Next to the TV in his trailer home sat a stack of videotapes piled high above my head. Every movie from the Black cult classic canon was somewhere in that stack, and on lazy Saturdays, when the tractor grew tiresome, we popped tapes in and stared until our eyes watered.

Without adults to report to, John and I acted up at Dad's place. Other than sparse warnings, we roamed wild. And in roaming wild, we emulated the man we idolized. Dad was a player. A rolling stone. He did what he wanted when he wanted, unencumbered by the responsibilities that anchored the other adults we knew. If he wanted to play soccer, he played. If he wanted to smoke weed, he smoked. If he wanted to feel special, he turned to one of the many women who flocked around him like a sweet aroma. We just wanted to be near him, to catch his cool by osmosis. It didn't matter that he didn't make time to come close—in fact, it added to his allure. He was so free that not even his own children could rein him in.

The only time we bothered Dad during the day was when we needed to eat. Even then, the interruption was brief. We tried to catch him in the spare windows of time when he wasn't interacting with customers or kicking tires. We said we needed to eat, and he handed John a few dollars to feed us both. We skipped down to the gas station around the corner and stacked up all the junk food we could for ten bucks. That sugar rush gave us the energy we needed to chase each other around through the evening hours. Come dinner time, the two of us split a Pizza Hut pizza. It was tradition.

On the rare occasions that we didn't eat pizza, we ate African stew. Though Dad left Nigeria, Nigeria never left him. He ached for home constantly. He reminded us how they did and didn't "do it back home" anytime he grew unhappy. Nigerian music played when DMX didn't. And he clung to his deep-rooted Nigerian tendencies, even when they clashed with the norms of his new home.

One Saturday afternoon, John and I made a new friend. A stringy, gray goat appeared on the lot without explanation, tied to the back of Dad's trailer. John and I had begged our mother for a dog for months. Here at Dad's, our prayers were answered tenfold—the only thing cooler than a dog was a goat to call our own. We named our goat Sparky, the same name we had chosen for the dog we never got. We tugged on his tail and fed him fruits plucked from the trailer park trees. We poked his snout and patted his belly. We fantasized about bringing him home. Playing with Sparky in the corner of the lot got old after an hour or two. We knew better than to free him, so we wished him well and wandered off to find other trouble. We chased each other around the lot and army-crawled beneath cars. We ran back to Dad's trailer when the sun got low, but Sparky was nowhere to be found. Dad wasn't living in the trailer at that point; he'd rented an apartment a few miles away. His assistant informed us that he'd headed home with Sparky already, and she could run us over when we were ready.

Walking up to Dad's apartment building that evening, we saw a bright red mass swinging from the corner of his entryway like a flaccid flag. Red goo dripped from its front hooves. We squinted from a distance to make it out. That was the body of a goat. A Sparky carcass.

A wall of exotic scents walloped us at Dad's apartment door. John twisted his face to hold back the tears. We didn't have much time to mourn before dinner. Dad fed us goat stew that night. It pains me to say it, but Sparky was delicious.

My relationship with Dad changed as I aged. Our shallow quality time lost its charm. As I entered my early teenage years, a boy beginning the long transition to manhood, I needed more. Just when I needed him, he receded.

Our visits to Dad's lot grew more infrequent. Over time, weekly became monthly, and monthly became "come back soon." He became even more unreliable. Occasionally, he showed up when he said he would. More often, John and I packed our bags, got dressed up, and waited in our mother's living room for an occasion that never arrived. Occasional missed visits turned to weeks and months without contact. He just disappeared. When he resurfaced, he didn't have an explanation for our past missed plans. He had two new pairs of shoes in his hands instead—bribes for John and me, to make amends.

Dad bought a large plot of land when I made it to sixth grade. It was everything he'd ever wanted—he could slaughter all the goats his heart desired and live unbothered by American customs. He moved the double-wide trailer onto this new plot and called it home.

By then, I was as much to blame for Dad and me not spending time together as he was. Dad lived in Durham, a little over an hour away. I was a teenager, and my friendships mattered to me. Plus, my friends showed me I mattered to them. The drive to Durham meant sacrificing time with people I loved to be unwelcome company for a man I barely knew. I avoided the trip whenever I could.

The first time I traveled to his new digs, I rode next to my mother in a huff. I didn't want to go, but she convinced me it'd be beneficial. She dropped me off and promised to return the next day.

The night began on a high note. Dad kept a few dirt bikes on the property, and I sped through his new acres for hours. Like the tractor years earlier, the motorbike was a risk I never would have been allowed at Mom's place. The childhood rush of being free from supervision returned. Jessica, Dad's latest girlfriend, stepped in to offer me dinner. Jessica had translucent skin that hung around her thin frame loosely. She behaved erratically and smelled bitter. I was never a fan. Hunched over the same large pizza pie I'd eaten for dinner a decade before, my mood started to turn. I was in the middle of nowhere with a man I didn't know. We had lived entirely separate lives, never living under the same roof, never exchanging more than polite small talk. He knew nothing about me. More than that, he didn't want to know anything about me. He kept to himself on my nights in his home. Every second I spent in his home was wasted—time that could have been better spent with my friends in Raleigh. When Mom picked me up the next day, I told her that I never wanted to return to his plot in Durham. And I never did.

Two months later, Mom entered my room with news to share. She waited for me to sit down before unloading. Dad was becoming a dad all over again. Jessica, his longtime girlfriend, was pregnant with their first child. I'd only just begun to react when Mom quieted me. She wasn't finished. Geraldine, Dad's assistant, was pregnant too. Dad had two babies on the way.

I nodded silently. Mom probed, but I'd receded too far into myself to even hear her words. She sounded muffled and distant. I just kept nodding. I nodded her right out of the bedroom. And as soon as she exited, I broke down into wailing sobs.

I didn't realize I had still held out hope for my relationship with my father until the last of it stormed away. He gave so little of himself to John and me. We saw him a few times per year and, even then, barely commanded his attention. Now, that fraction would be split up even further. Whether it was right or wrong, I felt like he chose to replace us. The news confirmed a suspicion I'd had all along—he never wanted us in the first place. It severed whatever was left.

I didn't become angry with my dad after that. I became apathetic. I numbed myself. I refused to be let down again by a man who had only ever disappointed. I moved on about my life. I matured through middle and high school independent of his example. He disappeared for months-long stretches. Fine. I never asked why. When he popped back up, I kept our conversations short. There was nothing for us to talk about.

On the few occasions I saw my dad in middle and high school, coordination went through Mom. If he wanted to appear for a sporting event or to drop off new shoes, cool. I wouldn't object, but Mom handled the logistics. That way, in the most likely event that he didn't show up, I wouldn't be disappointed.

Time pressed on, and I grew up and apart from my father. I creaked into adulthood uncomfortably and eventually moved away from home. I returned for holidays to reunite with Mom and John and, on rare occasions, Dad too. Every few trips, he got wind that I was in town and reached out.

Once, we drove the streets of Raleigh together, rehashing long-dead subjects and small talk, when he parked the car and lowered his voice. "I need to talk to you, son." There was a long silence after that. I looked at him, and he looked straight ahead. The vein on his neck bulged from the strain of selecting his next words carefully. "There was a reason I wasn't around much when you were younger." Another silence. Then, "I was locked up."

I watched the weight float from his shoulders after uttering those four words. I didn't realize I'd been holding my breath for the many minutes of suspense. I could barely breathe. Then he fell into the sentences that followed.

Dad grew and sold weed. A lot of weed. And it got him sent to jail. At least, that's what he told me. He was in and out of the prison system throughout my childhood. When months passed without word from him, he wasn't roaming the country on the fun tour I imagined or holed up in his trailer with lovers and vice. He sat in a six-by-eight cell, cut off from the world.

Anger was the only emotion I'd ever seen from my father. But in that car, he was all over the place. Sullen one moment, remorseful the next, explosive after that. His speech wasn't entirely coherent—it whiplashed from breathy explanations to hollered justifications.

It also wasn't an apology. Dad was tired of not having relationships with John and me. In his mind, he was owed his boys back. This was a last-ditch effort to reverse course.

I waited for him to finish, then I sat in silent thought for a long, long time. I hadn't felt anger toward my dad in years, and I still didn't. I pitied him. This man had nearly built a life for himself. He fled the violence of his home country and found safety, family, and honest work in America. But he never found peace. He threw all he had away. And now, in the downslope of his life, he clamored to get it back, but it was too late. I looked at him and saw a stranger.

In his speech, he turned himself into the victim of systems that were erected to hold him back. Everyone had it out for him, the police most of all. I wouldn't let him do it. I called out his misdeeds. Mistakes sent him to jail, but they were *his* mistakes, no one else's. And those mistakes left his teenage sons without a father. He still wasn't prepared to stare that ugly truth in the face.

My pity deepened when I considered where years of running

from the truth had led him. He had six children with three women—he and Jessica had two more after the first—and he didn't have a positive relationship with one of them. Geraldine had moved on. Jessica hadn't, but a years-long battle with drug addiction had rendered her unrecognizable. Still, if my father needed someone to talk to, he called my mom, the woman he'd lost two decades before. He was alone.

In time, that lonesomeness would only worsen. Jessica never did free herself from her disease. A few years after our conversation in the car, she succumbed to it. The courts removed their children from my father's custody. Four people vanished from his orbit in a snap.

America met my father for the first time near the end of my season of *The Bachelor*, but it didn't see him through my eyes. America didn't see his history or the history that lived between us.

The show forced me to confront the parts of our history that had held me back from diving headlong into relationships in the past. I had never given all of myself to a partner, and it was easy to see how my parents' past infected how I thought of love. I feared becoming for my wife what my father was to my mother. Dishonorable. Unreliable. A source of pain. I feared bringing children into the world whom I might one day disappoint.

When the show's producers

> I had never given all of myself to a partner, and it was easy to see how my parents' past infected how I thought of love.

suggested that my dad come on for an episode, I agreed because I thought the time had come for another conversation. We hadn't seen each other in nearly two years. I hadn't numbed myself as completely as I imagined. Our history weighed on me throughout the season and, for me to feel love, we needed to confront it.

Dad agreed for his own reasons. He didn't understand what he was walking into, and it showed. Mom tried to warn him that we would be in a place of raw emotion and vulnerability, but he didn't listen. Stubborn and mesmerized by the bright lights of television, he came to the Nemacolin resort in Pennsylvania, the site of my season, expecting to celebrate his son on a national stage. I spent the first half of the conversation just trying to work past his unrealistic expectations of our discussion, until, finally, the smile faded, and we spoke honestly as men.

Dad carried his own baggage into that encounter, just as he had throughout his life. He was fatherless at five years old. He saw violence and crime and flawed male role models at every turn. That doesn't excuse his choices, but it goes a long way in explaining them. He led a life of tragedy, and pain begets pain. Our damaged relationship was the outcome of years of few highs and many lows between us, and all those moments delivered us to that room together. America needed to understand that journey in order to understand where it spat us out. Without context, the conversation looked like a stereotype that too many are familiar with: the trope of the deadbeat Black dad. The label doesn't fit because it's one-dimensional. Dad and I contain complexities.

The conversation, including the parts that weren't shown, helped me overcome the limits I'd placed on myself. It didn't deliver us to a rosier place. But it allowed me to let go of the greatest fear looming over me. I confirmed I wasn't anything like my father. He matured without a father, and then history repeated itself. But it didn't have to. Abandonment isn't hereditary. I could break the cycle.

And in many ways, I already have.

My journey to manhood began the day Mom told me Dad had fathered other children. The news broke my heart. It thrashed away the last of the admiration I still held for the man.

From that day forward, I matured with intention. I wanted to be a better man than he was, and I searched elsewhere for role models to show me the way. I wanted to operate on principles. I wanted to be a rock for my family.

Years later, entering the conversation with Dad during *The Bachelor*, I believed I was fully formed. Well over a decade had passed since he last hurt me. I was an independent man now, strong of body and character. But it was an illusion. I was still shackled to my fears. I couldn't have the loving life I wanted until I confronted them. I couldn't be free until I confronted him.

> Abandonment
> isn't hereditary.
> I could break the cycle.

I reached a mile marker on my journey when I overcame my childhood trauma.

Growing up requires two essential elements. First is accountability, understanding that your life is your responsibility. That epiphany can come—or not come—at any age. Some twelve-year-olds decide to take hold of their lives and break the mold of their forebears. Some fifty-year-olds still blame others for their mistakes.

Accountability can only take you so far. Accountability looks to the present and the future, but to thrive, you must also look to the past and learn from it. That's the second—and most crucial—element. Grandpa was the first to teach me that lesson, and Dad reinforced it later. Avoiding past trauma only places a ceiling on your successes. When you confront those challenges head-on, you open yourself up to the blessings you deserve.

> Accountability can only take you so far. Accountability looks to the present and the future, but to thrive, you must also look to the past and learn from it.

CHAPTER 4

Chase What You're Good At

*Don't sit down and wait for
the opportunities to come.
Get up and make them.*
—Madam C. J. Walker

My jaw dropped the first time I saw a pantry. It was at Kyle Faltisco's birthday party. Fourth grade. When the bus driver inspected my note that afternoon and nodded that he'd pass my stop and drive me on to Kyle's, I felt like he'd punched my ticket to the great beyond. Finally, a thrilling break from the weekly routine.

The pool party was first on the agenda. Kyle came from—and lived in a neighborhood full of—large, loving, white families. A dozen of our classmates gathered around, but so did Kyle's older sister, and her friends, and all the neighbors and their young ones as well. We played Marco Polo and held our breath in competition until our lungs shrieked out for relief. In breaks, I camped out by the buffet table, gorging on shrimp cocktail hand over fist. I'd never tried shrimp before, and who knew if I ever would again.

As day faded to dusk, the party moved inside. Ms. Faltisco offered another snack to tide us over before dinner: "Oh, Matt, you still hungry? Just go grab whatever you want out of the pantry."

Pantry? I'd never heard the word before. I followed her finger to the kitchen and assumed I'd figure it out. Silently, while the family's backs were turned, I tugged on drawers and cabinets, searching for this "pantry" she spoke of. Only dishes and cutlery. The final place to search was a door, tucked away in the corner. I tiptoed over, but when I swung it open, I swear an operetta broke out overhead. I saw glimmering logos and bags piled high to the ceiling. Fruit Roll-Ups, Goldfish, and Lay's. Pallets of Gatorade in every color, stacked to my waist. And water bottles. Water bottles! The Faltiscos were much too civilized to drink from the faucet like we did back home. Their water was store-bought, pre-packaged, and sealed for portability. If an earthquake struck right then and buried me under a mound of processed goodness, I would have either eaten my way out or died happy.

I ate myself sick. I had one of everything—chips, chocolate, and candy—then returned for another round. There was no time to hem and haw about my swelling belly, though. We had places to be. Mr. Faltisco drove all the kids to Blockbuster—another paradise I'd only ever heard of—and rented new games and movies for us to enjoy. When we got back, hot pizza awaited us. Stomach still bursting, I did my best to pack it into what little real estate the Fruit Roll-Ups and Dunkaroos had left behind.

Riding high on sugar and wonder, I stayed awake as long as my body would allow me. When I awoke the next morning, I felt a hint of remorse that this dream ever had to end.

The overnight introduced me to the real-world impact of wealth—how its presence, or absence, shaped my experience. It was the first time I'd been exposed to that hard lesson, but it would not be the last.

In the years to come, new friends invited me along for too many sleepovers, fancy dinners, and family vacations to count. I joined enthusiastically, even if, as I aged, I felt hesitation as well. New friends always included that my mother was white when they introduced me, and approving nods followed. Eventually, I questioned why. I monitored the responses from their parents closely. Why did they beam with pride when I—a soon-to-be six-foot-something Black man—entered their sacred spaces? Only later did that question dig into me. When young, I was too wide-eyed and excited to slow down.

Years after the Faltiscos, the Buckleys would broaden the universe even further beyond my few square miles of Raleigh. Tim Buckley came from a full house of four kids, with two parents who seemed to love each other as fiercely as the day they met. Tim went to private school, but we met during Pop Warner football when we were little and stayed close through the years. His family was everything I wanted for myself—a warm, two-parent home with little to want for. He invited me to Sea Island, Georgia. I'd never been on an island before and had a slew of logistical questions: steamship, helicopter, or airdrop? Upon arrival, I stepped into a world of luxury beyond my wildest imagination. Everything from the frescoed ceilings to the marble floors seemed to be plucked from a world I knew nothing of but wanted desperately to discover.

From an early age, whether in the backyard a few blocks over or in vacation homes miles away, I found excuses to steal away from my friends to go sit with their parents. I so cherished the experiences these adults exposed me to, seeing a side of life that was hidden from my family's two-bedroom apartment. I wanted them to know I appreciated what they'd done for me. I wanted to be invited back. If my gratitude verged on kiss-assery, it was only because I knew I was there by their grace alone. And I desperately wanted to return.

While alone with the senior Buckleys and Faltiscos, I tried to unearth the keys to their success. What did they do for a living? What does that *mean*? What'd they do to get there? Did everyone at their office have houses like this? To their credit, they humored me. They got a kick out of the back-and-forth, breaking down the principles of entrepreneurship to a young child. For me, the conversations grew into something more than a scheme for future invites. I treasured the wisdom they shared, wisdom that no one in my family could have handed down. I wanted what these people had. And I wanted them to show me how to get it.

My relationships with the Faltiscos, Buckleys, and the Raffertys—whose son JP I played basketball with and quickly became one of my best friends in high school—blossomed at a crucial time in my life. Without realizing it, by the end of ninth grade, I arrived at a fork in the road. I'd soon be making the first grownup decisions of my life, decisions whose consequences would ripple out for years to come. No one in my family had properly framed those choices for me. No one placed any real importance on college. It was already clear that John, two years ahead of me, wouldn't be going on to college, though none of us knew just how far he'd fall before picking himself back up.

My mother didn't burden John or me with exceedingly high expectations. Of course, she wanted the best for us, hoped we'd achieve success one day. But there's a difference between hoping for success in the abstract and setting out clear markers to get there. College wasn't any more on her radar than it was mine. Mom wasn't familiar with the college admissions industry that had shot up since she was last in school. And on top of that, she was

busy—remarkably busy—providing for the two boys she was raising alone. Who could blame her for not dragging me down a path
she wasn't well acquainted with herself?

As a result, on the afternoons when I wasn't going home with
one of my friends, I was more than happy to return to our apartment and squander the day. Mom would still be at work and John
would be off with his friends, cruising around the neighborhood.
I had the run of the place. I skated all over the apartment complex
until the sun got low in the sky. When it did, I went inside and
played video games until my eyes hurt. Homework was rarely on
the agenda—I glided through the simple curriculum at Sanderson
High School with ease. Whatever the teachers had in store, I could
worry about it in the hallways tomorrow before class.

My teachers and mom were more than happy to watch me glide
through life as an A– student without so much as lifting a finger.
I brought home good grades, so I satisfied our unspoken agree-
ment—what I did with the rest of my time was my business. But
things were different in the Faltisco and Buckley homes. My friends
were exemplary students. I looked foolish goofing around while
they scribbled away at their advanced assignments. Their parents
noticed. Before long, they were on me, peppering me with questions about why I wasn't in any AP classes yet and which schools
were on my radar for life after Sanderson. They recalled the long list
of ambitions I'd rattled off for them in the past. How did I expect
to get there without putting the work in?

And it wasn't just the parents who dialed up the pressure on my academics. Unknowingly, Kyle and Tim did too. Listening to them complain about their classes, tossing around mathematical characters and twelve-letter words that I didn't yet understand, triggered my competitive instincts. I knew I was capable of anything that they were. Now, I felt I had to prove it.

Throwing myself into my schoolwork for the first time, I learned skills that would serve me well over time—diligence, perseverance, discipline. I fought my way into the classes that Kyle and Tim were in, and I excelled there just as I had previously. I learned important lessons, like hard work does truly pay off. But I never honestly believed that education could transport me out of our little apartment and into a four-story house like the ones they had.

The Faltiscos, Buckleys, and Raffertys granted me the first real vision of what a future fixed in success could look like. For years, their playrooms, emerald lawns, and, yes, pantries, remained the standard of true wealth in my mind. They were a tangible manifestation of the privileges they enjoyed, which I'd never known. They inspired in me a longing for more; I'd do anything I could to provide that life for my family. But I remained skeptical of the means they said would lead me to their end. Sure, they were all lawyers and doctors and entrepreneurs, but I wasn't like them. None of them looked like me. In fact, I had never met anyone who looked like me who had all that they had. Fortunately, just when they granted me a vision for my future, a path to grab it appeared before me.

By ninth grade, my body had transformed. I wasn't the same lanky boy I'd always been. My frame stretched out well past six feet, and new muscles wrapped their way around it. I suddenly had the body of a man.

As my body changed, so too did the way the world regarded me. Now when girls spoke, they added a newfound sweetness in their tone. They squeezed my arm flirtatiously by the lockers between classes and laughed deep belly laughs at my same jokes that weren't so funny just a year before. A flood of new attention is a dangerous thing for a teenage boy to receive. Pretty soon, you couldn't tell me nothin'.

Girls were charmed, and coaches were beside themselves. I'd always been athletic, traveling across states with Mom for track meets and AAU tournaments—I always stood out. But the growth spurt gave me a whole new suite of tools to work with. I jumped higher and ran faster, stretching out for casual acrobatics that would have astonished my younger self. On the field, I wasn't just good anymore, I was dominant.

The summer before I was to begin high school, I spent each afternoon underneath the sweltering North Carolina sun, fighting for a spot on the varsity football roster. If any freshman deserved a spot, I did—Sanderson didn't field a particularly talented group, and I'd run circles around kids for a full season. But nothing would be given to me, and summer workouts were a chance at a first impression with the men I hoped would become my coaches.

Unfortunately, I hadn't learned modesty yet. I treated the work-outs as a formality, dusting other kids in sprints when I had to make my point, but otherwise swaggering back and forth without much effort.

Weeks in, I hadn't had much contact with the head coach, but I assumed he knew my game well. How could he miss me? Then we collided, at last.

Another long, hot day of practice teetered to a close with sui-cide sprints—running back and forth on the field until you keeled over or the drill was done. Both seemed possible. Trotting into the finish, Coach called out: "James, you didn't touch the line!" Then, turning to the rest of the team, "Line it up. We're running it again. Thank James!" The other players grumbled and moaned, and I burned hot with anger. Muttering, but not so low as to be silent, I growled every curse word that came to mind. "What was that, James?!" Not as silent as I'd imagined. Coach cast me off to the locker room and told me not to bother returning for var-sity training the next day...but I couldn't take a step until I fin-ished the sprints I owed him. Such was my introduction to Coach Tindal. Soon, he would become the closest thing I ever had to a role model.

Coach Tindal was a clean-cut block of a man with a muscular jaw that he locked in a no-nonsense grimace. It was easy to imagine him, not long ago, suiting up in the same pads we did every day and thrashing players into oblivion. Tindal and his assistant kept an office in a glass cube in the corner of the school weight room. One side looked out over the gym, the other side showed the school courtyard, and the center presented a view of the weight room itself. It wasn't paranoia speaking when we thought he had his eye on us. Stepping into his office felt like trespassing—a boy passing into a man's world. If he closed his blinds, you knew you had trouble.

Coach Tindal also had a caring side to him that sat closer to the surface than it did for many of the other coaches. Coaching was more than a job to him; it was a calling. And he took seriously the responsibility of molding boys into young men of character.

It would take me some time to dig up that side of Coach, but once I glimpsed it, it was undeniable. I didn't spend long on the junior varsity football team—I outperformed the others and was on varsity after a game or two. There too, I shined, and when Coach turned his attention to me again, he delivered it with a softened tone.

Coach Tindal sat me down midway through the varsity season. "Matt, have you thought about going to college?" Nope, I hadn't. No James man before me had ever gone to college, and John had no plans to; it wasn't even on my radar. On the few occasions when it did come up, I labeled it a tomorrow problem—I was only a ninth grader and graduation seemed miles away. "Son, I don't think you understand the position you're in." Coach Tindal broke it down for me. He saw potential in my game beyond even the inflated skills I saw in myself. He knew my background by then, knew that

I wanted more for myself, and painted a simple choice: dedicate yourself to football, and anything you want can be yours.

Coach Tindal's directives were simple. Show up to practice every day, keep your grades up, and stay out of trouble. Commit yourself to this game and schools will trip over themselves to get to you. You can go to any school you want—and then he added the magic words—"for free."

Coach Tindal's speech stopped at college scholarships, but it gave my imagination the push it needed. It floated freely from there. If I was a high school star and *could* be a college star, then why stop there? The pros were nothing but a small hop from an elite college program. I'd look good in Panthers blue. Bright lights, screaming fans, and dump trucks of dollars for a mother and brother who'd spent too long on the harder side of life.

I told him I was all in.

With that conversation, Coach Tindal became the first adult I'd ever known to demand the best from me. No one had ever looked me in the eye and delivered the frightening and exciting news that the future was mine to mold. Many might enjoy my success, but only I would suffer my failure—my effort alone would be the difference between the two. He saw so much potential in me, beyond even what I saw in myself. I made it my mission not to disappoint the man who thought so highly of my ability.

Through the remainder of the season, the coaching staff didn't need to goad me into going the extra mile. I worked myself harder than they ever could. I was first in the weight room and last to leave, pulling and pressing dumbbells as though I were angry at the weights for betting against me. At home, I put down my skateboard—why jeopardize my future? Instead, I flipped through playbooks, committing movements to memory, learning the science of the dance.

I improved immediately. By the end of my first season of high school football, I was dominating on defense the way I had in middle school. Nothing compared to the feeling of throwing all of myself into something and watching the fruits of my labor grow. I fed off the thrill of competition.

> Nothing compared to the feeling of throwing all of myself into something and watching the fruits of my labor grow.

For the first time, I excelled at something, and I could claim it as my own. I'd grown used to not having a lot, looking to my classmates' lives and feeling as though I'd come up short. I didn't have the money they had. I didn't have the video games or the sneakers or the pantry with snacks to the ceiling. But I had football, and I worked myself raw each day to make sure that everyone—my teammates, our rivals, college coaches—knew that they couldn't take that from me. It was mine.

As I made good on my promise to Coach Tindal, the two of us grew closer. I showed willingness to invest in my future, and Coach doubled down on his offer to do the same. On weekends during the off-season, he drove me to football camps around the state, so I could show off my talents against the best competition North Carolina had to offer. On the journeys to and from, we talked about my game and how it had improved, but also my home life, my dad, and where I wanted to be in the world. Once, he asked me where was my dream college. College itself had only just become a dream—I hadn't gotten much more specific than that. Coach told me not to worry about it. Then he Googled the top one hundred schools in America and sent my game tape to the first fifty on the list. "Be patient," he said. "They'll come calling soon."

The following season, Coach added "wide receiver" to my list of duties on the team. I played offense and defense now. I rarely caught a moment of rest and continued to live up to my commitments off the field...almost. I never missed a practice, working twice as hard in the gym as many seniors on the team. I kept my grades up; Sanderson's curriculum was simple, so that was easy. But that last part of Coach's ultimatum—"stay out of trouble"—that part I struggled with.

One afternoon in health class, floating high off my own success and bored to death with the lesson, I laid a trap. A classmate removed his shoes for a demonstration and, while he stepped away, I funneled applesauce into them both. Once the deed was done, I stepped away inconspicuously and waited, snickering alongside my classmate. All class I tracked his movements—to our teacher, his desk, and back—silently urging him to return to his shoes at the front. My attention span for mischief was short, and I eventually lost interest, almost forgetting about the prank and letting my mind wander. We wrapped up the lab, and I gathered my books, but just as I did, a loud squelch erupted from the front of the class. I shot my glance upward to see the boy with a startled look on his face and applesauce oozing from the eyelets of his Nikes. The noise sent the class into fits of laughter. It also sent me to detention. Once Coach got wind of it, he sent me even lower—to junior varsity.

His decision was nothing short of catastrophic. Consider for a moment that football was my only lifeline then. I had nothing else. Football was the only skill that might enable me to transcend our humble home life and reach the plush life I so desperately desired. But, in a single instant, all my hopes of college and the world beyond were dashed as quickly as I'd dreamed them up. No colleges would ever see me on JV. Nothing would ever happen. And I'd never leave Raleigh.

The greatest gift Coach Tindal ever gave me was illuminating the path to my wildest dreams. His second greatest was taking it away.

I refused to sulk, though it would have been easy to. After more than a year of hard work, I was back where I began: on JV and invisible to the outside world. But I was too pissed off to despair. Pissed at the health teacher for snitching on me. Pissed at Coach

Tindal for coming down so hard. And, most of all, pissed at myself for squandering my first real shot at glory.

I injected all that fury into my play. My first game back on JV was against Cary High School. I didn't speak a word to the coaching staff, not even Coach Tindal, who'd come to see the game. We were expected to trounce the opposing side, so the JV coach rarely put me in. I didn't protest, sitting silently on the far end of the bench. The game was closer than anyone expected, and on the few occasions that I saw the field, I unleashed the fury that had been brewing within. An interception here. A sack there. A kick return for a touchdown. After each play, while others celebrated, I stalked back over to my end of the bench, refusing to even look at Coach Tindal or the others who watched.

As the final seconds of the game ticked away, the scoreboard showed our team down six points. The JV coach threw me back on the field, hoping to avoid an embarrassing loss. The quarterback barked hike, dropped back, then hauled up a prayer in my direction. I leaped, brought the ball down with my right hand, and threw the defender over my shoulder with my left. Once I turned, there was no stopping me; I was a locomotive pointed toward the end zone. We won by one point. And still, I didn't say a word.

The next morning, Coach Tindal didn't say much either as I sat across from him in his office. He didn't have to. He gave me the green light to return to varsity—the end of a short-lived punishment that felt like an eternity. I understood the moral of the story loud and clear—a lesson that has never faded. I had no margin for error. My dream could be snatched away from me in an instant. I needed to act like it.

The lesson came just in time—things were about to heat up. The game tape landed just as Coach Tindal said it would. The whispers in the hallways grew thunderous as groups of burly men in athletic polos with bright logos stalked over to the gymnasium. Tennessee, Alabama, Ole Miss—America's powerhouses. They pulled me out of class. They watched me run sprints and lift weights. They told me to spread my arms wide, so they could measure my wingspan, then to bring them back together, so they could inspect my hands. Sometimes, they grunted or nodded in approval. Often, they said nothing at all. Then they were off—it would be another group's turn tomorrow.

For a time, these intrusions were routine, so much so that friends, family, and Coach Tindal all had to remind me constantly that this was not, in fact, normal. Something special was coming together.

I received a call from Coach Tindal while walking to English class one afternoon in eleventh grade. He rarely called midday with good news. Looking at my phone glow, I racked my brain for my last misstep and a fitting excuse. "What's up, Coach?" He was silent on the other end. I waited for the barking to start. Then, "I just wanted to be the first to tell you, East Carolina has offered you a full-ride scholarship to come play for them."

Now I was silent. My mind blanked and my body numbed. A dream solidified into reality before my very eyes. So did a lump in my throat. I'd be the first James man to go to college.

"...You there, Matt?" Coach asked.

"Yeah, Yeah, I'm here, Coach." All I could do was thank him and smile. I called my mother from the hallway and heard the cracks in her voice as tears of joy streamed down her cheeks. "I'm so incredibly proud of you, baby."

A hurricane crashed down in the week that followed. Soon as one school stepped forth, the others flooded in. The next day I got another call from Coach: "I just got off the phone with Air Force. They want to offer you a scholarship to come play." The day after that, it was UMD. By week's end, West Virginia, Kentucky, Syracuse, Navy, and Virginia Tech had all sent me offers to consider. Harvard and Yale jumped in too; both told me I could have a spot if I retook my SAT.

By the end of the week, the question wasn't *if* I'd be going to college but *where*. I didn't know the first thing about any of them. I didn't watch college sports growing up and hadn't spent years fantasizing about university life like other kids had. They were all just names to me.

What I did know was that I wanted to stay close to Mom. I wanted her to come to my games and feel proud of the man she'd made. I consulted her on the decision I had before me. I sat down with Coach Tindal more times than I could count. After months flipflopping and schmoozing with coaches, I made my mind up. I was going to Virginia Tech. Mom assured me she would make the three-hour drive for gamedays.

There would be one final hurdle to riding off into the college experience I prayed for. I tripped over it while at Young Life camp, the summer before my senior year. The Christian sleepaway program didn't allow campers to keep cell phones during our weeks away, but I'd snuck mine in—flirting with high school crushes back home was well worth the risk. I'd only just decided to play for Virginia Tech and hadn't yet had a chance to reach out to the coaching staff. Before I could, I received a call from VT's offensive coordinator, while in between camp activities. He was brief: "Matt, a wide receiver just committed to our program, so we don't have a scholarship for you anymore. I'm sure things will work out elsewhere. Good luck, buddy." And then he hung up.

I thought committing was a formality. I didn't even know it was possible for an offer to be rescinded. Only moments before, I had commanded the driver's seat, determining my own fate. The call from VT let me know the limits of my control. Now that I understood the stakes of the game at hand, I couldn't let another opportunity slip through my fingers.

I knew my decision, and I called the position coach right then and there. Nervous and adrenaline-flushed, the acceptance tumbled out of my mouth. I'd become a Wake Forest Demon Deacon next year. But even as I hung up the phone with my future coach and felt the glow of accomplishment wash over me, I had no idea how that one decision would alter the trajectory of my life.

I learned two important lessons on the path from class clown to college. The first was the importance of clearly defined goals. I'd known I wanted better for my family in an abstract sense for years, but the Faltiscos and the Buckleys were the first people to provide me a clear vision of what "better" looked like. My interactions with both families spoke to the crucial role that exposure played in shaping my future. It is one thing to say, "I want to be rich enough to provide for my family." What is rich enough? What does "provide" really mean? An apartment, or a house, or three houses, a supercar, and a yacht?

It is an entirely different experience to point to a pantry and say, "That will be mine." The latter goal is concrete. It empowers you to chart a concrete course to achieve it.

The second lesson was the value of hard work and commitment. There is something almost indescribably satisfying about achieving a goal that once seemed unimaginable. You could fill entire libraries with the books that profess to have secret recipes for success, but their processes have always seemed foreign to me. Mine is straightforward: 1) Set a goal. 2) Determine a path to that goal. 3) Work your ass off 'til you get there. Find a talent and

> There is something almost indescribably satisfying about achieving a goal that once seemed unimaginable.

refine it until it's a skill that sets you apart. And when success trickles in, never forget that it can vanish in an instant. Work harder.

My drive has always come from a simple place: create a better life for my family. For that reason, I was thrilled about Wake Forest, but I wasn't yet satisfied. Next stop: the NFL.

CHAPTER 5

It Could've Been You

But by the grace of God I am what I am.
—1 Corinthians 15:10

I blacked out in those first moments after I heard the news. All Mom heard through the phone was an agonizing shriek before the line went dead. The neighbors heard the scream too; they soon called Mom to tell her to rush home ("Someone needs to be with Matt. We don't want him hurting himself."). I'd already left by the time she arrived, headed off to retrieve the car from the parking lot where John abandoned it. I looked at the car, still running, and imagined the event as it happened. I sat in his driver's seat for a long while before pulling off, feeling his essence in the still-warm vehicle, straining to summon him back to where it all went wrong. The next time I saw my brother, he was a prisoner.

There was nothing fated about the way our paths diverged. Looking at him on the two-way, closed-circuit camera feed at the penitentiary, I didn't know how to process the man I saw. He looked so vulnerable, powerless to the whims of correctional officers and the law. He'd only ever been powerful in my eyes.

In my first memory, John is protecting me. I couldn't have been more than a few years old. The memory presents itself as a series of snapshots, like an old-school slide projector. I see Mom and Dad fighting in the home we shared. I can't hear their words, but I feel them; the shouts rattle my insides. In the next image, I'm outside, my eyes are cast down and I'm playing footsy with an anthill. It's dark out. Shouts still ring out, but they're muffled now. John stands above me, arm around my shoulder, standing between the house and me like his body can contain the yelling.

My memory skips a few years before picking up again. It starts in earnest in my grandparents' house. My parents had just separated, and my mother set about constructing a new life for herself and her young boys. John and I stuck together like Frick and Frack. When we weren't chasing each other around our new palatial home, we explored the neighborhood that surrounded it.

The house just across the road was home to Mrs. Young and

her sons: Brad, Ben, Brody, and Brent. The four B's. They'd found themselves in a similar position: they too were recent uproots following a soured marriage. If we were trouble, the four B's were terror. We watched them from our grandparents' front yard and longed to join in. John mounted the courage to stomp over and introduce himself long before I could have. It was in his nature to be social.

The four B's became our first and fastest friends. They swept us up in their tornado, and the six of us tumbled through the neighborhood. Wrestling in front lawns, high-diving into leaf piles, showering in garden hoses. If I made the mistake of challenging John, I lost. The contest didn't matter. Taller, stronger, more charming, and better looking, John was the further evolved version of me and the bridge to all my first friendships. It didn't stop at the B's; John kept me in tow on school playdates and neighborhood adventures. My childhood was a time of freedom and fun. I have John to thank for those memories.

A year passed, Mom got back on her feet, and we moved away from our grandparents' house. She chose an apartment less than a mile away from her parents' place. The three of us had space of our own now—tiny, but ours. It was time for me to go to school, which meant it was time for me to board the bus, which meant it was time for me to enter a world run by kids and try not to drown. John was my protector. As much as he was a bridge to some, he was a shield from many others.

On the first day of school, I stood at the head of the school bus aisle and suffered glares from every row to the last. The bus had prison rules, and the older kids were enforcers. They punked me early. Each seat I stepped up to, I was greeted by a shaking head and fingers pointing to the back where the busted-up rows were. I sunk low in submission. John didn't. He barked at kids two or three years older than he was, "Ayo, nobody talks to Matt like that 'cept for me." By the time he was done, every seat in the joint was open to me. I took my place near the front. Nobody punked John's little brother.

The conflicts escalated when we got older, but John came battle-ready. In the early teenage years, any excuse for violence was a good one. I was a lover, not a fighter, but growing up among John and his older friends, I knew how quickly a joke could turn to blows. Wannabe macho men establishing dominance the prehistoric way.

I was twelve the first time I *almost* fought. John and I traveled to Hoop Heaven, a basketball camp that had earned its name in our minds. We loved the long days of competition and early morning training sessions that made us feel like soldiers in the army of ball. But most of all, we loved the escape. Hoop Heaven was in upstate New York. Our mom had finagled a scholarship for John and me that brought the camp within reach, and three summers in a row, we escaped North Carolina for a few weeks to see another corner of the country.

At the end of a long day of basketball, some campers went to the concrete courts behind our cabins to continue playing—the early hours were pleasure; these games were business. I crossed up a preppy older kid earlier in the day, and he challenged me to a game of one-on-one to get his revenge. He checked the ball and we began. First possession, I crossed him up again, drove to the basket, and leaped for an easy layup. I was still soaring through the air when his elbow jabbed my ribs, sending me flailing to the ground. Prep wanted a fight. I looked up from the ground to see him standing over me, fists clenched, ready to go to work. Just as he wound up to swing, an orange object fell from the sky, crashing into his head. John came flying in and tackled Prep before he could swing around to react. He'd nailed Prep's head with the basketball to stall the fight. When John was done with the boy, he turned to me. "I got you, bro."

In the early years, doing everything together meant travel soccer and rec league basketball. Later, it meant jobs. John wanted to work as early in life as the state would allow. He was too prideful to ask Mom for spending money, and she wouldn't have had much to share even if he had. So, at sixteen, he went to work.

John took every odd job a teenager could land. He was a bus boy and a camp counselor and a locker room attendant. When I was a teenager, beginning to think about jobs of my own, John worked at a Halloween store. The store only popped up for two months of the year then vanished again, but for those months, John's job was to make sure customers came in. The company put him in a different costume each day and instructed him to stand on the curb and dance. He had to dance well enough that paying customers wanted to join in on the party.

For weeks, after football practice, my friends drove me the long way home so that we could pass John at work. We spotted him from two blocks away. A Harlem-shaking pirate. A two-stepping teddy bear. A wizard, walking it out. Every day, we laughed so hard, the sight brought us to tears. John was in his own world. He possessed a crucial quality that made him perfect for this job: he couldn't have cared less what anyone thought. I envied John and the fun he had, not to mention the money he made. Next Halloween, I got a job at the costume store. I didn't have the courage to get out there and shake it, so I worked at the checkout inside the store instead. All season, from inside the store, through the masks and cotton cobwebs, I watched John—a robot doing the robot.

John and I navigated our family relationships the same way we handled every other part of our lives—together. I never remembered a time when our parents were together, but John did. He clung to those memories, even as they fell further into the past. We both admired our dad in our younger years. We saw the life he had, coming and going as he pleased, constrained by nothing, not even his own family, and envied it endlessly. That was real freedom— a feeling too sublime to imagine for young kids with bedtimes and spankings to contend with. But John's admiration of Dad ran deeper than mine. There was something about having been alive for a time when Dad was the man of the house. They were only a few scant years, but they were enough for John to idolize Dad the way any boy wants to look up to his father.

John used to get giddy about our time with Dad in the past when it was offered. We both did. An outing with Dad meant driving the forty-five minutes to North Carolina State for his weekly pickup games. He'd discovered a whole community of Nigerian immigrants in North Carolina and got invited to their men's league soccer games. I never saw my father so happy as when he was storming around the field, chasing the ball and hollering out curses in his mother tongue. He found a slice of home on that field. I smile when I remember those games, despite the complex emotions I feel for the man. We all deserve joy.

The games were not, however, the father-son bonding "sesh" that we'd been sold. The commute was our time to catch up with Dad. He entered game mode upon arrival, and we were on our own. Sometimes we stayed to watch the old men frolic. More often, we explored the campus, striking out on adventures of our own creation.

We once stumbled upon the loading docks to what must have been the school's cafeteria. The place looked industrial and therefore was likely off-limits. We grinned. Adjacent to the dock stood the massive machinery responsible for heating and cooling the building—giant metal blocks ten feet tall each. They whirred noisily, creating a whooshing, vibrating shout that was felt as much as heard. John and I stumbled over to investigate.

If you took the access ramp to the corner of the loading dock ledge and looked down, you stood just above these steel towers. What looked, at ground level, like an impassable hunk of steel was actually several separate units organized in a grid with a cement wall encircling them all. The pattern created deep ridges between the units that looked, from above, like a labyrinth. We decided to treat it like one.

John went first. He hopped into the hole and threw his arms and legs out to catch himself on the metal walls, then eked his way to the floor, dropping down when close enough. I followed suit but couldn't catch the hot metal walls and fell to earth ungracefully. Once we made it to the floor, we chased each other around in rectangles. John clasped his fingers into little guns and took aim at me. We fired on each other simultaneously. Then we both fell to the ground, crying out in agony and laughing hysterically.

Heat radiated off the metal walls and made the trench sweltering. After only a few minutes of play, we were panting and had soaked our clothes all the way through. It was time to get out of here. We wobbled over to the spot where we had dropped in and stared up at the ten-foot concrete wall. We hadn't preplanned our escape route when we dropped into the trench. Now, we realized there wasn't one. The tops of the air conditioning units stretched well above what either of us could reach, and we were trapped on all sides by the cement exterior wall.

Panic gripped me immediately. I hollered out for help but could barely hear my own voice above the noisy fans. Surely, no one else could hear me. I scratched at the heated metal grates. An hour passed. Dad would be looking for us by now. The sky lit up in pink and orange as the sun sunk low. I couldn't help but wonder if we would die in this hole.

While I spun myself into a tizzy, John grew determined. He didn't shout out exasperatedly like I did. He planted his feet and hands on the walls and tried to climb his way out the way he came. When that didn't work, he hopped from wall to wall, ninja-like. When that didn't work, he ran at me full speed and told me to lace my fingers and hold them low to give him a boost. Failed scheme after failed scheme, as the sweat poured down, he kept trying, never discouraged.

After two hours of bouncing off the hot walls, John had a new plan. He told me to crouch low and he climbed onto my shoulders. When I lifted up, he summitted the metal mountain. No sooner had he gotten to the top than he turned belly down onto the steaming metal and reached for me. My brother dragged me out of the hellish trench.

Then we faced a different devil. My dad's temper rested on a hairpin trigger. The slightest infraction could send him into a frenzied, shouting tirade. And keeping him waiting for two hours was no slight infraction. He was scouring the campus in that very moment, no doubt worried about his boys. Finding Dad meant surrendering to whatever he had in store.

John tried to take the blame. He said it was his fault that we'd ended up marooned in the trench. My father agreed—John was the oldest and should have known better. Then he whipped us both anyway. Just like AAU basketball, neighborhood tussles, and school buses, John and I took our ass whippings side by side.

And the beating didn't color how we thought of him. John still idolized the man, and I still wanted to share in his life. When it was time to return to the field a few weeks later, we volunteered for the ride eagerly. We treasured what little time we had with Dad.

But already, at eight or nine years old, John's feelings toward our father were turning complex. Dad was gone most of the time. He was unreliable all of the time. His absence inflated into this great, unavoidable colossus. Other kids had fathers at home, and we didn't. Despite our admiration of the man, that was really the only fact that mattered.

John inherited Dad's temper. And in angry flashes, Mom caught the brunt of it. I remember more than once, John hollering out across the apartment, "You're not our real mom! Our real mom is in Africa somewhere. Give us back to her!" He knew better, of course, but Dad had suspended us both in such an uncomfortable state of uncertainty. Mom's never-ending care, plus the fact that she looked nothing like us, made her an easy target. She accepted his lashes with grace, seeing them for what they were—the protestations of a young, confused boy.

In middle school, when I gravitated toward sports, John

underwent a series of changes. I stepped into my role as jock and, to a lesser extent, class clown. John went the other way. He moved forward into high school, but years of poor performance caught up with him. John had a learning disability that held him back from excelling in class. Reading comprehension was incredibly difficult for him, and algebra could have been written in Russian as far as he was concerned. Sanderson didn't know what to do with a kid who learned differently, so they stuck him in rooms with the other kids they deemed unteachable. For a few weeks, John sat alongside kids with serious mental handicaps, being fed knowledge at a rate well below what he was capable of. He hated it. My mom wouldn't stand for it. She moved John to a private, Christian school slightly farther from home. So began the game of musical chairs that would see John attend five different high schools in four years.

While his academic career entered limbo, his athletic career ground to a halt. John had always seen sports as his only path to a better life, but for him, that path never led through college. It was big leagues or bust. He never imagined that academics could be a stepping-stone to college and whatever opportunities might stem from it. Early in high school, a broken foot sidelined him for an entire season. Academic ineligibility followed closely behind. He still played sports recreationally, but all at once, his dreams of going pro imploded.

His second stop on the school hopscotch tour sent him to Durham to live with our dad. He piled into the same double-wide trailer I'd begged Mom not to make me visit anymore. John still maintained a closer relationship with our father than I did, and Mom had grown exasperated, unsure of what to do with the son who couldn't sit still in class.

Love wasn't the main reason John agreed to live with Dad. Freedom was. Dad had too much of his own life to worry about John. He left John at home for long stretches while he was out, traveling to visit brothers or sweethearts. When he was home, women paraded in and out of the trailer. Only three years after John left, Dad would be convicted and sent to jail for possessing massive quantities of marijuana. I've never asked John what he saw while living in that trailer, but I've imagined.

John's time with Dad ended in an inevitable fight—a clash between the unstoppable force of Dad's rage and the immovable object of John's stubbornness. Once, Dad was driving John back to our family apartment in Raleigh when John responded to one of his questions with a snort. Dad exploded at what he saw as the ultimate sign of disrespect. John bit his tongue—the two were still many miles from home, and John knew Dad wouldn't hesitate to pull the car over, kick him out, and head right back to where he came from. When the car finally pulled up to our place, he hopped out, ran around to the driver's side door, and swung at Dad. The two had it out in the middle of the street. John moved back into our apartment later that week.

John's school tour eventually brought him full circle. He was back at Sanderson for senior year. I was a sophomore then, and college had materialized as a real possibility for life after graduation. Only question marks awaited John. I knew he wasn't destined for college, but what opportunities could possibly be in store for a Black man in Raleigh with only a high school diploma to his name? Was he destined to keep working the same odd jobs he'd taken up forever?

During his second stint at Sanderson, John fell into a different crowd than the guys he hung around with before he left. I knew the new guys by name and reputation.

To the new guys, John was "wheels." Our dad had given him one of the beaters off his car lot, and John rolled it around Raleigh with the windows down and the music up. The car granted John freedom and power—very few others had their own way of getting around. The new guys needed rides, and John needed a crew to call his own. The car brought them together.

I didn't know any of John's new friends well, and that was by design. I stayed at Sanderson through the years that John spent hopping around and, in his absence, watched those older kids grow into young men. I heard the rumors that floated above them— petty crime and gang affiliations. They showed me love even before John returned. I was a standout on the football team by then. After games, they strolled over and called out to me, "You balled out tonight, my man. What's good with you now? Want to go for a ride?" I wasn't interested. I pointed to my teammates and told the guys I was straight. I was a man on a mission then. Whatever it was that that group was getting into, I didn't want any part of it.

John graduated, and his future didn't get any clearer. He stayed at home with Mom and me and kept working the local restaurant job he'd been at for months. His new crew stayed nearby too, and they grew closer. They embraced John, and he embraced them right back. They filled out the back seats of his sedan and rapped along to the lyrics blaring out the speakers all night long. Occasionally, they stopped at the mall or convenience stores along the way and made off with what they could. Candy, sneakers, clothes. It was all fun and games to them. Then it was time to upgrade.

They planned to rob Jersey Mike's. The sub shop was fifteen minutes from our apartment and usually only attended by one employee who doubled as sandwich maker and cashier. John would drive the group at night and stop just outside the entrance. He'd sit in the driver's seat with the car running and in gear. The other two would don masks and storm into the restaurant. They'd demand the cash from the register, plus whatever was saved up in the back office. They'd take it all. They'd dash back to the car. John would speed off before the employee even had a chance to call the cops. Simple. They added a toy gun to the mix—a pellet shooter that looked like a genuine nine-millimeter—just in case the cashier felt stubborn, brave, or both.

On the big day, everything went according to design. They got the cash. They got away. But they made a mistake. One of the guys in the crew lived a block away from Jersey Mike's. After a few hours of laying low, John circled back around to drop his friend off at home. He returned to the crime scene in the same car with the pellet shooter still sitting on the back seat. When the police stopped the crew, they didn't need to call Sherlock Holmes to piece it all together. At eighteen years old, John pled guilty to accessory to armed robbery. The crime sent him to prison for six months.

Movies didn't prepare me to visit my brother in prison. I expected a vast room with high ceilings and families gathered around tables dotting the floor. I expected men in orange jumpsuits shuffling to and from their visitors, wrists and ankles cuffed. I expected to nod to the instructions not to touch the prisoners, then hug my brother anyway. I expected to console a brother who needed it.

In reality, a prison visit is a videoconference. My mother and I drove to the penitentiary and then huddled into a cubicle to stare at a screen. Somewhere else on the compound, my brother also huddled before a screen and, after a pause, a camera beamed him into sight. He was dressed in blue, not orange—first myth busted. He also wasn't alone. Behind John stretched a line of other men waiting their turn to see and hear—but not touch—loved ones.

The small talk that followed was bizarre. John remained stoic. He asked about relatives and football. We talked sports. He asked how my college recruiting was going. I gave him the abbreviated version. I didn't ask about life inside; the answers to those questions seemed obvious. We tiptoed around the likely few-hundred-feet distance between us that felt like an unbridgeable moat. Despite my plans to remain strong, I collapsed into tears. I couldn't bear to see my brother shelved away from the world. John's face hardly broke.

Later, after he'd been released, John told me about the need to remain strong in the eyes of the other inmates. Any show of vulnerability would have been understood as weakness. Weakness would have been punished. So I was the one that needed consoling during our visits, not John, and I'd get it from my mom on the ride back home—even sympathy was too tender an emotion to live behind the prison walls.

With the other inmates nearby and it being impossible to have honest conversations in front of them, John wrote me to let out his truth. In letters, John told me about the day-to-day difficulty of life inside, the constant danger and guardedness. He explained the larger difficulties of feeling stowed away and apart from the world. I felt abandoned, and he felt ashamed. He included sketches of him roaming the outside world, or of the two of us together as children. I reciprocated with action shots of me in my last game. For years, I carried a bundle of his letters with me in a backpack wherever I went. They contained the only honest moments we shared during the six months he was away. Eventually, though, I had to get rid of them. They carried much more pain than pride.

John was released from jail in time to see me walk across my high school graduation stage, but he wouldn't stay out for long. Between the ages of eighteen and twenty-five—his early manhood and my college years—John swapped freedom and incarceration the way he once hopped between schools. While free, he found it hard to gain meaningful work and reconnected with troublemakers that he knew before. New missteps would punch his return ticket to prison. Through the years, he fell out with many of our family members—relationships strained by the constant back-and-forth. They didn't understand how their kin could repeatedly make such life-altering mistakes. They couldn't bear the burdens of grief or guilt.

As John's stints away stacked up, I visited and wrote less. I regret that now. I justified it then by telling myself that some things were more important; for example, when I made it to the NFL, I could help everyone, John included. For the time being, I needed to numb myself from anything that could sidetrack my march to glory, even my own brother.

In reality, I just couldn't adjust to the sight of him in that jumpsuit. The thought of him languishing while I was out enjoying life crushed me. So I chased the thought away whenever it snuck up on me. I spared myself the pain of seeing him locked up.

Hearing his stories now, how he endured weeks on end at times without hearing from his loved ones, I marvel that he made it out at all. I wish I had had the strength then to give him what he needed— love and an open ear.

John was released from jail for the last time when he was twenty-five. He's been out in the world for almost seven years now and has kept his nose clean. But spending his formative years behind bars created changes in him that have lasted well beyond his sentence. He's a man now, a far cry from the boy who entered prison at eighteen, and the scars from his time away are ever-present.

He's quirkier now than he was before. For one, he's obsessively neat. John's room is spotless and sharply organized, just like his cell once was.

Sit next to John during a meal and watch a cyclone suck a plate down. No one eats faster than my brother. We teased him for it at first: "Slow down, bro; it ain't going nowhere." It was an adaptation he made while inside—food could be a cause of conflict; better to eat it all before someone came calling for what was his.

John still has a taste for state cakes. In the months after his release, he added graham crackers, honey buns, Oreos, and jelly to the shopping lists. Once in hand, he crushed the ingredients up and mixed them together to create the dessert he once made from commissary supplies.

Some changes were darker. John, already reserved, became more insular. He's a stronger, more serious man. And his Christian faith has entirely evaporated. During one stint inside, he became close with the Muslim brotherhood, and for a time, it appeared that he might commit himself to Islam. That too proved temporary; he is entirely atheist today. He is deeply spiritual but doesn't commit himself to any religion. Of the many changes in John, his faithlessness hurts my mother the worst.

I feel different. John is working through his trauma and hardship, just as we all are. He's finding his truth, and if that path takes him away from his faith, then that is how it must be. I'll continue to pray for him. I'm proud of my brother. He has turned over a new page in his life. He's back in Raleigh, doing honest work and building a career in music. He's come out the other side of the prison system strong and committed to his family. He's put the worst of his bad days behind him.

I often think back on our lives, our shared childhood and dissimilar adulthoods, and marvel at how things turned out. John was the better of us. When we were children, John was faster, stronger, better looking, and more charming than I could have hoped to be. We were brought up in the same way, faced the same challenges at home, and clinched the same victories on the court. Ninety percent of my young life was spent by his side.

As we got older, the differences in our personalities grew more pronounced. John was the more introverted of us. He was quicker to anger. But still, anyone would look at the two of us then and see brothers destined to share a path into the future, just as we had for the first decade and a half of life. I think on that similarity, that closeness, and wonder seriously how to explain the difference in our outcomes.

It isn't nature or nurture. It isn't a tendency toward good or bad that either of us has. It's simpler than all that. I think the difference could just be luck.

I am a few inches taller than John. My times on the track were a few seconds faster and I always jumped a little higher. I formed special bonds with special coaches at a pivotal time in my development. Athletics provided for my college education. Athletics drew mentors into my orbit and gave me relationships that spanned race and privilege. It could just be my athletic gifts—largely God-given—that led me to Wake Forest instead of a darker place.

Biographies and self-help books are always quick to lionize the protagonists. We love our heroes. It feels good to believe that we control our own outcomes. We as humans aren't quick enough to acknowledge that so much of our life path is totally, maddeningly, uncomfortably out of our control. John taught me that lesson.

Once you realize it, though, your mind can only go two places. The first is empathy. I felt so deeply for John's plight because he's my brother and I love him, but also because I knew I could *be* him. Any potential that was once in me was in him as well. He's responsible for his choices as I am mine, but mine were made easier by a few chance encounters. How could I judge him when I know the long list of blessings I've received?

The second is gratitude. Nothing is more humbling than knowing that I am not solely responsible for where I've gotten. I work hard. Incredibly hard. But sometimes the difference between success and failure is the flip of a coin. When you realize that, you can't help but feel grateful for the position you've been placed in.

Today, I do all I can to be a good brother to John. I need to show him the depth of my love. Twenty-something years on, the roles have reversed. I am as protective of him now as he was, and is, of me. I received blessings he never did. Now, my job is to be the blessing he never had, to provide him with access and opportunity, the way they were once provided to me.

Nothing is more humbling than knowing that I am not solely responsible for where I've gotten.

CHAPTER 6

Failure Sucks, but It's Necessary

Success is to be measured not so much by the position that one has reached in life as by the obstacles which he has overcome while trying to succeed.
—Booker T. Washington

My gut knotted as we stuffed the car with packaged goods that Mom mistakenly thought I'd need. Then we were off. With each mile that passed, closing the distance between Raleigh and Winston-

Salem, the knots grew tighter. By the time she wheeled our car onto Wake Forest's campus, I thought I might implode.

What had once been a distant dream, a borderline impossibility, rose from the horizon into brick colonial structures and pristine white columns. College was just as I'd pictured it would be. The sheer scale of the place stunned me. The lawns were boundless— rolling green grass stretching as far as the eye could see in every direction. Stand in any given spot, and everything you laid eyes on, except the clear blue sky itself, was called "Wake Forest." I had visited once before, but this time was different. This time I belonged. I was a Wake Forest Demon Deacon now.

The campus was missing only one thing: students. It was still July, time to report for fall athletes, and the Southern sun pushed temperatures well past ninety degrees. I didn't mind. I stared too intently at all the life ahead of me to notice the sweat soaking my back, until a plastic moving crate slipped right through the slick of my palms and crashed to the floor. Embarrassment. Double take to check for onlookers, potential friends, already lost. No? Continue on then.

I piled my stuff into the dorm building that would temporarily house the entire football team as one. I met my roommate—Tanner Price, starting quarterback for the Demon Deacons. This felt like freshman year of high school all over again. The uncertainty. Timidly feeling my way through each conversation. Imagining myself as a guppy in this vast new pond. Tanner claimed the top bunk that first day, and I wasn't one to get in his way. That first night, we stayed up trading war stories of high school glory. They were only days old, but already, nostalgia seeped into our recall.

Our team hit the weight room together on day one before we ever touched the field. I don't know if Coach intended to intimidate the younger guys early on. If so, he was effective.

My frame had filled out by the time I arrived at Wake Forest, but it did so more or less naturally. Yes, I worked in the weight room, but given the small scale of Sanderson's program, I'd done so without the professional-grade diligence that high-caliber programs across the country applied to their athletes. At Wake Forest, I was a boy among men. Linemen and defensive ends stepped up to the stand, then hauled Olympic-level weights above their head with an earth-quaking roar. The team gathered around to cheer on final sets that I couldn't dream of budging. Gazing around the room at those assembled, I saw lions, tigers, and bears. Everyone had been a high school standout. Everyone was the best athlete they knew. I wasn't at Sanderson anymore.

It soon became clear that I would not be the dominating force in this group that I had been only months earlier. In practice, I kept up. I made plays occasionally and held my own with the older guys. But I didn't stand out. In the weight room, I lagged far behind the brawny bodies on our team. Coach sat me down before summer session closed and informed me of the plan going forward. I'd "redshirt" this year—an NCAA designation that meant I'd sit out of playing for the season and retain four years of eligibility. I could still attend meetings and practice alongside my teammates, but when game time came, I wouldn't even put pads on. I'd stand on the sideline with the other unproven prospects for the entire season to come. I didn't bother arguing with Coach because I didn't have any firm ground to stand on. I saw the same evidence he did. I wasn't good enough to play with that squad yet.

While my experience on the field suffered, I felt for my groove socially. Those summer preseason workouts—hours together under the beating sun followed by team workouts, team dinners, and team outings—had their intended effect. The time together brought me close to other players who I'd move through Wake's hallways alongside over the coming years.

Kevin Johnson emerged from the pack early. Soon, we'd spend nearly every waking hour with each other. I had met Kevin during my official visit to Wake Forest a year earlier, and my first thought then was "This kid must be in the wrong place." Kev was all of six foot one, 155 pounds—a twig compared to the bulky beasts roaming campus that day. I didn't have to wonder long, however. During the light, padless workout we had later that day, Kevin put on a clinic in fast-twitch reaction time and athleticism. When I returned to campus one year after that first visit, his was one of the few familiar faces to greet me in the early days, so we gravitated to each other. At preseason, we clicked immediately.

As freshmen on the team, Kev and I withstood the petty hazing side by side, and it drew us close to each other. It wasn't long before we were tethered to each other, marching to practice, dorms, and back in lockstep. Our friendship made the preseason weeks, which were trumped up as some of the hardest we'd face, a breeze. Students trickled back onto campus, guiding tours and opening campus stores. The trickle became a flood, as everyone rushed back to campus living in the week before classes started. It was time for the team to move out of our temporary housing and integrate with the other students. And wouldn't you know it, on a sprawling campus with dozens of dorms across hundreds of acres, Kevin and I landed in the same building.

Our rooms stood two floors apart, but the steps were a formality. Kevin essentially lived in my room that first semester. Every day was the same as the last. In the evening hours, we roamed the dorm's halls, joking, flirting, and sniffing for trouble where it hid. We returned to my room by midnight. It was game time. You could find us huddled on the floor, shouting at the TV and each other, slaughtering zombies and maneuvering NBA stars until dawn.

Our grades suffered. We both missed more classes than we made, too tired to rise for mid-morning econ lectures. Frankly, I didn't care. I was a college kid now; my time was mine to spend as I saw fit. Thankfully, our play didn't suffer. Mine didn't because, well, I didn't play, was forbidden from touching the field on gameday. Kevin's didn't because he was a freak of nature.

While my football career at Wake Forest started off rocky, Kevin's was a rocket. From my seat on the sideline, I watched my new friend dominate. Off God-given ability alone, Kev ran faster and jumped higher than almost anyone I'd ever seen. He played cornerback, tailing opposing receivers like their shadows as they streaked up and down the field. I cheered as he swatted away pass attempts from guys whose names I'd read about online for years. He was a starter on the team from the moment we arrived on campus.

Kevin had another leg up on me from our first day at Wake Forest, besides his sheer skill on the field. Unlike me, he wasn't alone. Kev's closest friend from high school, Mike Campanaro, chose to play for Wake Forest the year before we did. In fact, he was the reason Kev committed to Wake in the first place. So, from our first days, Kev had an ally to show him the ropes—in football and the social scene. Fortunately for me, like Kev, Mike was a generous, likeable guy, and an easy addition to our party of two. The three of us became inseparable.

Also like Kev, Mike was a monster on the field. He played wide receiver, like I did, and with the benefit of an extra year on the team under his belt, separated himself as one of the standout talents.

Watching those two operate during my first semester on campus, I discovered the limits of my own commitment to the game. I'd long prided myself on my dedication to football; it delivered me to Wake. But I was nothing like Kev and Mike. These guys were addicted. Hardly a minute passed in each other's presence that football wasn't mentioned. They could name at least twelve guys on each professional team and another handful at every major college program. They approached their craft like artists, watchful for dips and flares in others' performances that they could steal for their own. In quiet moments, I watched the machinery behind their eyes crank on football fuel. It could've been intimidating if it weren't so inspiring. But there were few outlets to channel this new energy into from my spot on the sideline.

By the following year, the many nights that Kev and I spent gazing at the TV screen finally caught up with us. I nearly flunked out, clearing the low GPA requirement needed to retain my scholarship by the slimmest margin imaginable. Kevin paid an even steeper price. His poor performance in the classroom had made him ineligible to play football. And even though I was technically eligible to play in games my sophomore year for the first time, it didn't matter. I still didn't excel the way I had always envisioned I would one day. I grew frustrated with my stunted progress and did little to climb out of the hole I'd dug for myself in the classroom. Sophomore year came and went, and I felt my dream of an illustrious NFL career slipping away from me. With summer approaching, I formed an ultimatum. I'd give football one last shot. I'd move to Maryland for the summer to work with Mike's brother Nick, a trainer in their hometown. I'd commit myself to my craft and construct a body that could go to battle with the most fearsome players across our league. If next season didn't pan out, I would find another path—maybe football just wasn't meant to be.

Maryland was a *Rocky* training montage. Or a military training ground. Six days per week, we subjected ourselves to a Spartan regimen. We reduced food to its component molecules—protein and carbohydrate building blocks for the body we needed. Ground beef, eggs, sweet potatoes—unseasoned, cooked well, and measured by the pound. Nick trained me in the weight room and Mike's other brother, Vinny, taught me how to box. Within weeks, my body swelled, and I continued slopping muscles onto my bones like they were wet clay.

Kev and Mike showed me around their hometown on our days off. I'd spent two years hearing about the people and places that had molded their life histories, and at last, I had an opportunity to see it all for myself. Though I lived with Mike's family, it was Kev's home life, and the plush surroundings of his youth, that made the greatest impact.

Kev was as unassuming a guy as I'd ever known, appearing most places in the same raggedy sweatpants and Nike sweatshirt that he'd worn the day before. And college life in Winston-Salem had a leveling effect on most students, despite our varied backgrounds. There just wasn't much stuff to spend money on. Everyone on the team had the same meal plan, and on weekends showed up to, and were often turned away from, the same frat parties. But I always suspected Kev came from money.

For starters, his parents flew to every game. That alone separated them from most—not everyone can hop on a weekly flight just for a few hours of football. The man I watched cheer from the crowd, Kevin's father, had a presence about him that I simply hadn't seen in a Black man before. He commanded the universe. He strode with a self-assuredness that just oozed "I'm a boss."

More than all that, though, meals were the biggest tipoff. All the athletes had meal plans, the golden ticket Deacon Dollars that could be traded for all-you-can-eat goodness in the school's dining hall. I was, and had only ever been, broke. I also was, and had only ever been, hungry. Facing an opportunity, for the first time in my life, to eat my fill day after day, I didn't know how to act. I ate my way into stomachaches, went to bed, woke up, and did it again. I was just ecstatic to have calories to pad my stomach with, but even I could admit that the meals weren't great.

Chipotle was a delicacy I could rarely afford. I would have eaten it every single day if I could have. On the rare occasions when I did, there were always opportunity costs to consider. What would the meal mean for gas money that week? What if I had a date come up (I never did, but *what if*)? Chipotle today meant sacrifice tomorrow. I stuck to the free food that Deacon Dollars bought me.

Kev, on the other hand, never worried. He said yes reflexively, without the telling pause that separates the college kids who were broke from the herd. When I came to stay in his home for the first time and laid my eyes upon the suburban mini-mansion that rose up before me, questions ricocheted around my mind at lightning speed. We were close enough by then for me to ask.

Kev's father had started a commercial interiors business years earlier, before either of us were born. The business flourished in Baltimore and soon spread around the country, garnering Kevin Sr. millions and furnishing Kev with the plush lifestyle that lay before me, the only way of life he'd ever known.

Just as I had with the Faltiscos, Buckleys, and the Raffertys before him, I soon peppered Kevin Sr. with the questions that bubbled up in my mind. But this time felt more significant.

Raleigh's wealthy families showed me the heights of what privileged life looked like. They inspired envy; I wanted all that they had. But I was never one of them, and I never honestly believed I could be. I didn't look like them. Their example showed me the end, but not the means. Watching them, I doubled down on my investment in football. After all, the only men with lives like theirs who looked like me were on the TV screen, rapping or catching touchdowns.

But here, before me, was a Black man who had achieved all the same success as those white families, and he'd done it by playing their game. Mr. Kevin Sr., and the time we shared, planted in me the first seeds of a novel concept: maybe I could succeed without football.

That thought, however, would need desperation to bloom. For the time being, I had tunnel vision for the task ahead. Wake Forest gave me a scholarship that could have gone to some other deserving soul. It was time to show them that their risk was worth it.

I played in my first game as a Demon Deacon during my second eligible year at Wake. I was an all-star in preseason that year, throwing around my added weight well enough that the coaches took notice. Finally, in the first game of the season, it was my time to shine. The moment I'd worked toward for either months or a lifetime, depending on how you count it. And that night, under the lights and on the biggest stage I'd ever set foot on, I played absolutely terribly.

This problem would nag at me throughout my career—I was a practice standout and game time flub. My ability and athleticism had risen over the summer, but my confidence on the ball hadn't followed suit. And in the heat of battle, confidence was 90 percent of what mattered. I dropped a few passes and returned to the bench for game two of the season.

The relegation was short-lived. My replacement got injured in the next game, giving way to a chance at redemption. Game three, I was back on the field.

Our quarterback heaved the ball my way in the second quarter. I leaped up and pulled it into my chest. Like that, I caught my first game-time pass since graduating high school. Landing back to earth, I turned to see green space ahead. I chased after it, eyeing the promised land just fifty yards ahead of me. I wanted it. Forty yards and closing. Still plenty of room to run. Thirty-five. Thirty. Twenty-five. I could smell the glory now.

I looked to my left just in time to glimpse the Mack truck bearing down on me. Then it blew through me. I felt the burst of a bullet instantly. Pain radiated out through my neck and chest—far-reaching and unbearable. I rolled in the grass in agony. My collarbone didn't survive the hit. First successful play and first injury all in the same seconds. Out for the rest of the season, just like that.

All I wanted to do was compete. Just when I'd gotten good enough to do so at the highest level, my body began failing me. The collarbone went first, but many other injuries followed. I would never play a full season of Wake Forest football.

If the season after my summer in Maryland was meant to test whether I still had a professional career ahead, the universe answered loudly: "No." It was time to move on to something else. I would still play and seize opportunities when they appeared, but I had to start laying the groundwork for a plan B. I needed to dig my GPA out of the ditch I had buried it in.

I'd spent enough time with my friends' parents by then to finally grasp the opportunities that corporate life offered. I didn't have any interest in the commercial interiors world that was Mr. Kevin Sr.'s domain, but I still wanted the prosperity he'd earned. I wanted to be rich.

The year was 2013, and though America had mostly shaken off the financial crisis, everyone still carried the fresh lessons learned from the worst recession in modern times. The headlines of that era gave me a whole new vocabulary. Collateralized debt obligation.

Leveraged buyout. Initial public offering. I didn't know what any of it meant, but I knew the people who commanded that language wore pricy watches and tailored suits. I had several friends in the business school at Wake Forest. While I had been off in Maryland honing my skills, they were in New York City, working internships at century-old institutions. And when I returned to campus to a season cut short, they returned with their pockets full, having made more money during a summer in the city than some folks in Raleigh made in a year.

I spoke to an academic counselor about transferring into the business school. She was kind not to laugh me right out of the room. My two-point-something GPA wasn't getting me anywhere near the finance department. I chose the next-best thing, economics, and tried to muster the same intensity for this new pursuit that I'd once applied to football.

Over the next two years, I drew all I could from the college experience I'd been gifted. I hit the books hard. I finally adjusted to the pace of Wake's workload. This wasn't Sanderson, where showing up was 85 percent of the battle. I unlearned bad habits. I revived my grades. I used the football alumni network to land internships at a few of the same big-name banks that my classmates flocked to New York for. I decided to become an investment banker.

I found my groove academically, but my social life was weak. Outside of Mike and Kev, I made a couple other close friends, but not many. I didn't achieve the big-man-on-campus status that I assumed would transfer over automatically from high school.

My race was, for the first time, a serious impediment. Entering Wake Forest, I shed the goodwill that I'd built up with families over a lifetime in Raleigh. White kids no longer looked to me as the exception, the palatable Black friend they could bring home to meet the parents. I didn't look biracial, so no one knew I was. Nobody mentioned my white mother when introducing me anymore and, now that they didn't, I understood why it bothered me that they ever had. Benefits evaporated away with my whiteness. I was treated like any Black kid at Wake Forest, which is to say I was treated like I didn't belong. I was all but locked out of mainstream party life, created by and for the white Southerners running the frat circuit. Girls that might have given me a chance back in high school looked the other way when I passed them on campus. I heard the n-word more than once.

But along with the bad came a more significant good—I fostered more honest relationships. Mike, Kev, and a few others saw me for who I was, not who I wasn't. I didn't get bonus points for defying their wrongly held stereotypes. We were on the same footing, trying to make it through college side by side and negotiating the challenges that stood in our way together.

> I was treated like any Black kid at Wake Forest, which is to say I was treated like I didn't belong.

Kev and I dealt with a similar discomfort. Kev's privilege in Baltimore bought him entry into white spaces that were forbidden to us both at college. Rejection became routine. Friday nights, we'd stalk about the campus, pointed toward a party we'd heard of, or listening closely for the rumbling bass of one we hadn't. We'd find some frat house with coeds spilling out the front and step up to join in the fun. There, a white kid a third my size would turn us away, regurgitating a line we'd heard dozens of times before. The answer wasn't "We don't want Black people at our party." It was "no athletes," or "no more guys," or "brothers only" (which, in practice, was no different than "whites only"). If we stuck around long enough, we'd undoubtedly see a group of baseball or lacrosse players, square-jawed and white-skinned, step up to that same doorway and stroll in with smiles and hoorays.

Maybe the frat boys were just arrogant. Maybe they didn't want strangers in their home. Maybe the guy-to-girl ratio was just too perfect to toy with. Maybe…but I doubt it. We couldn't have hollered out racism at much that we saw on Wake's campus. But we were put out so often in our college years that both Kevin and I felt sure there were bigger forces at play.

Eventually we stopped trying—we didn't want to be where we weren't wanted. We gave up on Wake Forest and extended our network, driving hours to East Carolina or UNC or University of South Carolina in search of parties that wouldn't act so burdened by our presence. At nearby High Point University, we met Shane Handler, a short, Jewish kid who dapped me up smoothly and unironically introduced himself as Gucci Shane. "You serious?" I asked, "Like Gucci Mane, but Shane?" Gucci Shane blinked twice in confusion, "Yes...what do you mean? That's my name." We've been friends ever since. He was the first to show Kev and me the side of college life we'd seen in movies—the carefree release that we longed for. We bounced between High Point parties, flirted with High Point girls, and ended the night with pizza at sunrise. The grass looked greener over there. We wondered why we ever chose to spend the best years of our life in an institution that hadn't made space for us.

Mike Campanaro was the first of us to go. And he went big.

My fourth year at Wake Forest, I flew down to Miami to join Mike and his family for three days of parties, beaches, and sunshine. We had a lot to celebrate. Mike had been drafted to the NFL. The lifetime of work he'd invested had finally paid off.

The three days of the draft felt excruciating for Mike, and almost equally so for those of us who loved him. Mike balled out during his years at Wake Forest, never changing from the tranquil, understated character he'd always been. He played well enough to get into the conversation in professional circles, but his fate was far from guaranteed. There were dozens of talented receivers across the country. Mike was on the cusp.

After not hearing his name called the first or second day of the draft, we entered the third and final day with our blood pressure boiling. Mike's turn came in the last round. The Baltimore Ravens selected him with the 218th pick. Mike was headed home.

Whatever sadness I felt at seeing my close friend leave campus, it was overshadowed by my unbridled excitement for him and the journey ahead. Mike had been of a single mind since even before I met him. He gave everything to football. I felt privileged to have had a front-row seat to his work ethic and ultimate glory.

As Kev and I entered our final year at Wake, I glimpsed the faintest glimmer of something new: hope. During my middle years of college, plagued by injuries and a lack of breakout ability, I'd all but given up on my football dreams. The coaches had too; they spoke about my football career in the past tense before I graduated like a eulogy to my dead potential. But my final year brought a surprise—a new coaching regime stepped in to lead the team.

My relationship with the old coaching administration had soured by the time I was an upperclassman. We weren't outwardly hostile to each other, but I couldn't escape the feeling that they viewed me as a failed investment. I felt the disappointment oozing from their lectures, and it sucked away my motivation. I brought value to campus in other areas, but in football, my reason for being there in the first place, I hadn't contributed. I fell into a funk.

I was back on campus in the summer of 2014 for my final preseason with the team, stepping through the motions of a training program that felt aimless, when Coach Dave Clawson and Coach

Kevin Higgins, the new wide receivers' coach, called me into his office. Coach Higgins was silver-haired, clean-cut, and callous, with the tight-lipped grimace I'd come to expect of lifelong football guys. He had the characteristic bluntness too. Coach Clawson sat me down and gave it to me straight: "Look, Matt, the last coaching staff didn't have much good to say about you." He paused to let his opener land. "I'm sure you're a nice guy and all. But you've been unproductive on the field these last three years. The former staff suggested I reallocate your scholarship to someone else that can do more for the team." Again, a pause, this time long enough to think it was my turn to plead, "But sir, I..." He waved me off and continued, "I disagree with their assessment"—a heaving sigh of relief—"but I do need to see more out of you."

"You've got all the potential you've ever had, but your clock's near run out. If you want this, work at it. There's no such thing as on time anymore—either you're ten minutes early, or you're late. Work your ass off this summer and show me something, and you'll get your shot on the field. You control your destiny now."

His speech reminded me of the similar one Coach Tindal had delivered years earlier. Coach Clawson gave me a blank slate to work from. I shrugged my shoulders and felt a weight that I hadn't felt in a long time: expectation. I'd always risen to the occasion in the past. I didn't plan to stop now.

I balled out my final season. I became a starter, and my play was soon a key factor in our path to victory. Coach was right, the potential was always there, but I was short one piece: confidence. Confidence was the difference between a practice all-star and a gameday hero. My senior year, after four years of watching from the sidelines, I discovered my confidence. And success flowed from there. Late in the season I had one more injury to contend with—a broken hand courtesy of a cornerback at Louisville—but it didn't matter; I'd shown my stuff by then.

> Coach was right, the potential was always there, but I was short one piece: confidence. Confidence was the difference between a practice all-star and a gameday hero.

My performance that year re-inflated a dream that I had considered dead. I played just well enough to make space for hope—there might be a professional career in my future after all. Things were far from guaranteed; it would take a few good workouts before the scouts and a whole lot of luck, but I'd fought my way back into the conversation. That alone was a blessing.

Agents reached out to me that spring, offering to usher me along the path ahead. I didn't hear from the big-time guys, but I felt flattered nonetheless. I eventually settled on one. While Kev and other top-flight prospects from around the country flew off to destination training facilities in preparation for the draft, I spent even more time in the Wake Forest weight room. No agent was coughing up airfare for such a speculative prospect when Wake was free.

I spent day one of the 2015 NFL draft in the cheap seats of the Auditorium Theatre in Chicago. I was there in a support role. From my spot up above, I spied the Johnson family gathered around their own banquet table, clutching each other's hands nervously. For Kev, it wasn't a question of if his name would be called in the first round, but when. Electricity coursed through the air that evening. Soon, a whole new crop of athletes would ascend to the pros—and my best friend would be among them.

The household names went first—Jameis Winston, Marcus Mariota, Todd Gurley—no surprises there. In the middle of the round, we heard the words we traveled for: "With the sixteenth pick, the Houston Texans select Kevin Johnson." Kev floated to the stage while America watched. I jumped up and screamed from the balcony. Tears of joy streamed down both his parents' faces. After all the hard work and sacrifice, he'd made it. He'd be a millionaire by midnight.

From the Auditorium, we moved to the afterparty—the most joyous haze of a night any of us had ever had. Mr. Kevin had flown 2 Chainz out to perform, and friends new and old shook to his lyrics. The next morning, my cheek muscles would need recovery from smiling so many hours on end. I couldn't have been happier for Kev—no one deserved it more. But as the party rollicked on, I felt a small tinge of remorse too. There's nothing easy about watching your dream come true for another.

I flew home to Raleigh the next morning and painstakingly

watched every remaining minute of the seven-round draft from my mother's couch. I pounced on my phone each time it rang. It wasn't logical to think I'd hear my name called from the stage, but NFL dreams don't live by logic. I didn't leave home for days after the final pick. The miracle I had counted on never materialized.

I had two long shots left. Through my agent, the Carolina Panthers invited me for a tryout. The New Orleans Saints did too. Both times I showed up to a field and saw eighty-plus guys who were just as big as me and just as skilled as me vying for only two spots. Only, by then, something had changed. I no longer wanted it as bad as the others did. For that reason alone, I didn't stand a chance. I showed what I could, but my heart wasn't in it. At the end of each day, the coaches read out a long list of names, punctuated with a simple sentiment, "Thank you for coming. You're dismissed." I stewed in disappointment too long to fall further. I collected my things and drove back to Raleigh. Football wasn't meant to be.

I returned to where it all began: Raleigh. No money. No prospects. A far cry from the future I stretched toward for ages. By any measure, I failed.

It is impossible to see the value in failure when you're cooking in it. The death of a dream is like the death of a family member. It felt like a piece of me, no different from the heart in my chest or the breath in my lungs, was snatched away forever. I mourned the loss of my life in the bright lights for a time, wallowing in a well of self-pity and regret.

Fortunately, hindsight grants both wisdom and perspective.

As I look at the arc of my life beyond that low point, the many other dreams and journeys that have come and gone since, I'm grateful to have learned early on what it meant to throw myself fully into a pursuit. Some might look back on a similar journey and end result and say, "I wish I'd worked harder at a plan B from the outset." I feel exactly the opposite. I treated football as my only lifeline. For a time, it was. And I'm grateful that I trained myself to erect blinders at an early age.

No matter the dream—athletics, architecture, or astronomy—there comes a time when nearsightedness, singularity of purpose, is all that separates good from great. For multi-talents, used to hopping between pursuits, that sort of focus takes adjusting. Some never do.

My football journey was valuable precisely because it ended in failure. It taught me the mix of desperation and nearsightedness I'd need to apply to whatever I chose to chase down next.

When I eventually did climb out of the hole that I found myself in (spoiler alert: I did climb out of the hole that I found myself in), it was the depth of that hole and the height of the climb that gave

> No matter the dream—athletics, architecture, or astronomy—there comes a time when nearsightedness, singularity of purpose, is all that separates good from great.

the journey meaning. I no longer had to wonder what rock bottom looked like. I fell from Wake Forest and crashed down with a thud. In a perfect world, perhaps I would have coasted off the graduation stage into accolades, fortune, and fame. But that path was not meant for me. And standing here, the man I am today, I know I needed that glimpse of anguish. I cling tighter to the blessings I do have. I'm grateful for every day that I wake up even slightly better off than I was the last.

CHAPTER 7

Get Back Up

*I've missed more than 9,000 shots
in my career. I've lost almost 300 games.
Twenty-six times, I've been trusted to take
the game-winning shot and missed.
I've failed over and over and over again in
my life. And that is why I succeed.*
—Michael Jordan

Resilience" sounded like a noble ideal befitting the period of my life that followed college, but it only makes any sense in retrospect. If you'd asked me in the moment, "I'm broke as hell" would have been the more fitting phrase.

After graduation, I boomeranged back to where it all began: Raleigh. I was down on my luck. I carried my college crates back into Mom's house. She wouldn't let me go hungry, but she wasn't going to put any money in my pocket either. I needed to find work. While Mike Camp and Kev were flying high with their professional football teams, I braced for a crash landing.

First step: find a job. I'd worked my entire life, from the time John and I first held down our childhood jobs. Searching for work in Raleigh wasn't new to me, but it was *because* it wasn't new that I dreaded the process. I wasn't afraid to find an honest hustle and work hard at it; I just could not believe that, after five years away, rubbing shoulders with the future elite, peeking into new worlds of knowledge and experience, I'd fallen back to square one. Why did I ever bother to leave at all?

My job hunt led me to interview with a temp agency based in Raleigh. John had worked with the company regularly to find work since his release, and he suggested I use it as a starting point. The woman who greeted me at the office was warm and inviting in a way that both comforted and nauseated me. I delivered her my résumé and she educated me on temping. Each week, she would send out a list of odd jobs available in Raleigh and the surrounding area. I could pick any one I wanted if it was available, which would place me on a one- to three-week-long contract with the client. When the contract ended, I could pick a new one or continue on.

The most common position available on the list was "porter," which was more a classification than a trade. A porter was a utility tool. Real-estate clients used the catch-all term to refer to the people who tended to all things that needed tending to on their properties. The role sounded simple enough. First up, I was a porter.

I quickly learned how the temp agency used polite words to obscure bleak job descriptions. My first day on the job, managers referred to me as both a porter and a "cleaning assistant" and directed me to scour the apartment complex grounds for "excrement or anything that might sully the outdoor experience of our residents." I reported to the groundskeeper shed, and the team equipped me with antibacterial gloves and plastic baggies before translating my job description to plain English.

The complex had an issue with residents not cleaning up after their pets in public spaces. I was the solution. I was a shit picker-upper. My sole purpose on the property was to pick up shit. A human pooper scooper.

Each day that week and for two thereafter, I rose early, reported to the groundskeeper shed, and received fresh equipment for the day ahead—new gloves and bags. Then I roamed across the property to search and destroy. I marched crisscrossing patterns along the complex's web of walkways. I found shit on sidewalks. I found shit on grass. I found shit on shit. And each time I encountered the enemy, I accomplished my sworn duty. The world was a more sparkly, less shit-riddled place thanks to my important work.

I once ran into an old classmate from Sanderson while walking about the apartment complex. He had dropped out before graduation, unable to resist the big figures the streets offered him. I smiled and called out a hello. "What you been up to lately, man? It's been a minute." He called back, "Oh you know, same old." The sun glinted off the chain around his neck and caught me in the eye. My eyes darted down reflexively and landed on his crisp Jordans. Then he chirped back up, "How about you, brotha? Heard you went off to college." I shook my head. "Oh, you know…" I looked down at the baggy and my soggy Vans. "Just picking up shit, man." He paused, eyes scanning my outfit and the surrounding complex behind dark shades, then, "Don't miss any." And he walked off.

After a few weeks, I got my first porter promotion. I was off poop watch and on to fire watch.

For some reason that is still unclear to me, maintenance turned the fire alarms at the apartment complex off between seven p.m. and seven a.m. each day. For safety and liability purposes, the company needed someone to patrol the grounds to ensure that nothing burned while the systems were down. That was the job—walk around a building in the middle of the night making sure it hadn't caught fire. You can't make this up.

I showed up for work each night and stalked the hallways. As part of the job, every fifteen minutes, I recorded my findings:

11:00 p.m.: No fire.

11:15 p.m.: No fire.

11:30 p.m.: No fire.

11:45 p.m.: No fire.

12:00 a.m.: Still fireless.

Weeks of fire watch and not a single blaze slipped past my watchful eye. I was a natural.

The only perk of life as a porter was the flexibility it allowed. I selected jobs that worked around the training regimen I'd set for myself. When others asked, I said I was training for another shot at the NFL. Perhaps that was true. But I knew by then that my chances of making a roster were slim bordering on impossible. The larger truth was that I didn't know what else to do with myself. I'd only ever been a football player. Letting go of the game meant letting go of my identity. I couldn't relinquish the one part of my life where I felt security.

I only enjoyed one job during my time as a porter. After fire watch, the agency placed me at another apartment complex in Raleigh—a collection of nondescript brick buildings encircling a large swimming pool. I was to stand guard as pool security. Let the movies tell it, lifeguards deserve all the glory. They're the ones who get slow-mo shots and summer romances. But trust me, an industry insider, when I say pool security is where it's at. While lifeguards were cast off in their ivory thrones in the sky, weighted with real responsibility for real lives, I was down at sea level, chatting with swimmers and sunbathers as I pleased. As long as no fights broke out, I was doing my job.

Finally, a job I could enjoy. I watched football highlights and viral videos on my phone. I completed bodyweight workouts in the grass. I flirted with the girls who lined the pool deck. And I pocketed the money I so desperately needed.

This portering job was about as good as it gets for a temp agency. Then, an unexpected visitor appeared. I stood in the grass, joking with some guys I'd met earlier that day, when an ex-girlfriend from my time at Sanderson approached. We both looked up and caught each other's gaze simultaneously. She blurted out, "What are you doing here?" I hadn't seen her since high school, but she looked just as good as the day she dumped me. Persian girl, slender figure and bulging brown eyes. Jet-black hair that reflected the sunlight. She nervously fumbled with a set of keys in her right hand and hugged a paper bag of groceries in her left. I stammered, "I...You...ugh... You live here?"

Just then, a man about my age—barrel-chested with military posture—swaggered up behind her and tugged the groceries from her arms. He nodded to me, "'Sup, brotha," then, "You good, babe?" She grinned smugly, and the two floated off to the apartment they shared. After my shift, I returned to my childhood twin bed to rest my head.

I needed to get out of Raleigh.

I escaped on weekends. Mike had a year in the NFL under his belt and had played a few games. I was back home for his second season and fled to Baltimore to stay with him every chance I got. I scraped together the money for a flight when I could, but it was often out of reach. If I took the bus, the weekend would be nearly spent by the time I pulled into Baltimore. Usually, that left driving as the only option. The road trip would be an adventure in and of itself.

The ancient Chevy Trailblazer I drove wasn't even worth the rust that spilled off of it. It was a junkyard scrap pile that my father had rescued to give to me. I appreciated the gesture, but he should have just put it out of its misery.

I did everything in my power to avoid making the nearly six-hour journey to Baltimore in my car. But when I didn't have the money for a flight, I made the trip anyway. The promise of time away from Raleigh was worth the risk of the road ahead. More than once, the car broke down before I ever saw Baltimore.

If I wasn't visiting Mike in Baltimore, I was visiting Kev in Houston. As a first-round draft pick, Kev reached celebrity and riches the moment he arrived in his new home. He lived the life young athletes dream of. Kev played every game his rookie season and started in most. He tackled and intercepted dudes with marquee names that he'd only read in sports sections for years. And off the field, he splurged on a few of the luxuries that any twenty-something clamors for.

Both Mike and Kev kept me around for no reason other than their caring spirits. They knew I couldn't afford to keep up with their new lifestyles. Before trips to Houston, Baltimore, or on one occasion, Vegas, I told them straight up that I was on my last dollar. I'd have to miss the luxe weekend ahead.

I only ever got one response: "Shut up and buy a flight." When the check came at the end of the night, they shooed my hand away and covered my portion. They wanted me to experience all that their hard work had given them, and our weekends away opened my eyes even further to the possibilities ahead. They showed me generosity and loyalty, and their successes fed my ambition.

Kev invited me to my first Super Bowl the year it was played in Houston. I wasn't quite at my lowest at that point, but I was close—still far too broke to even dream of making the trek alone. As a hometown player, Kev had the hookup for all the best parties all weekend long.

Super Bowl weekend is a spectacle that has to be seen to be believed. The glitz and glamour of it all was astonishing. The blinding shininess. I'd grown used to running in the same circles as athletes, including a few high-profile ones. They were Kev's peers, so we often crossed paths while out around Houston. But Super Bowl weekend brought together household names from every industry. Actors, models, rappers, idols of every size, shape, and description. Tailing Kev, I couldn't get from my hotel room to the car outside without an involuntary sharp inhale at the sight of yet another star who lived inside the TV. I was like a kid at the zoo for the first time, ogling exotic species I'd only read about in storybooks.

The night before the big game, Kev arranged for us to attend an exclusive party at a club in Houston where Migos would appear as the special guest. I was a massive Migos fan but never caught them on the few occasions they came to Raleigh. I was near giddy for the night ahead.

We rolled to the club as a crew—four or five sizeable Black men, each more athletic than the one before him. To the untrained eye, I might have looked like I belonged. Look closer, though, and wonder how the hell I stumbled into this circle. These guys dressed in designer silks and soft imported fabrics from Italian labels. Diamonds dripped off their wrists and bedazzled their necklines. I slid into a pair of beat-up Vans and the same vintage flannel I'd worn through five years of Wake Forest frat parties. Not quite the same.

At the club, a hostess escorted our group to a table in the VIP section. I learned the disaffected strut from these guys, the stroll across the club that treated our path like a catwalk. We got to the table and assumed our positions. Drinks flowed. New friends gathered round. Then the Migos took the stage.

I kept it cool throughout the night, but the Migos cracked my façade. The first low note of "Bad and Boujee" oozed out of the speakers, and the trio stormed onto the stage, sunglasses low, even in the blackened room, and every color in the rainbow reflecting off their clashing outfits. I was hooked. I jumped up and down to the beats and rapped along through the first three tracks.

On the fourth track, each member of the group pulled stacks of dollar bills the size of cinder blocks out of their jackets and began throwing them into the crowd. Green confetti covered the sky and floated to earth fancifully. My jaw dropped. Everybody in the crowd continued bobbing their heads, still entranced, but unfazed by the money raining down. I glanced over my shoulder at the guys I'd come with. Each one was too caught up in conversation to notice the riches that covered the sky. I looked skyward again longingly.

These are the tests of character they don't teach you about in grade school. "Act like you've been here before" had been the motto circulating in my head since my plane first touched down in Houston. But there was new information to consider. I paused. As I did, a wad of cash landed on the table next to us, but all I saw was a full tank of gas. A flurry of ones in the air looked a lot like a flight to Baltimore. A woman brushed thirty singles—three Chipotle bowls—off her booth to take a seat. Would pride prevent me from grabbing what could so easily be mine?

Nope.

I slipped away from the table without notice and weaved my way to the middle of the crowd. I stood only feet from the Migos but turned my back to them now. I looked left. Looked right. Then dove to the floor.

I crawled on my hands and knees through that damn crowd,

avoiding stilettos and ignoring knees to the ribs. Club sludge covered my palms. I fished for wet dollar bills and stuffed them into my pockets when I found them. Every so often, through the forest of shins, I saw another guy stooped down on the same mission. We avoided eye contact. Shame had us both.

We emerged from the club a few hours later, and I finally got a look at myself in the light of the lobby. My jeans were damp and caked with grime from the knees down, but that wasn't the worst part. My pockets bulged out a few inches in each direction like a chipmunk with stuffed cheeks. It looked like I had football pads on.

When we got back into the car, I climbed into the back seat and sat in the middle. Now I was shoulder-to-shoulder with Kev's teammates; thigh to thigh. Soon as they got in, they noticed the small pillows pushed up against their legs. I stared straight ahead but watched the gears turn in their heads in my peripheral vision. I sighed as the whole thing clicked in their minds.

All at once, the car burst out laughing. They poked the poufy lumps on my legs. "Aye, Kev, you ain't tell me your boy was a stripper!" I sunk as far into the back seat cushions as I could. They laughed the whole way to our next stop. By the time we reached the afterparty, tears streamed down everyone's faces.

Altogether, I collected ninety-nine dollars. Kev said he would have paid me a hundred just to leave it alone.

By the fall after graduation, it was time to make a change. I hadn't yet made it to the Super Bowl, but I'd seen enough of my friends' lives to want more for myself. I couldn't continue to sulk over the loss of the life I had imagined. I had to start living the one I had.

I set aside football for good at that point, forcing myself to turn away from the "what ifs" that still lingered. I redirected the time and energy I spent on the game into my new path: a career in finance.

> I couldn't continue to sulk over the loss of the life I had imagined. I had to start living the one I had.

The foundation I started with made me more fortunate than many. Despite having near nothing to my name, I still had a bachelor's degree from a great university to lean on. I'd studied a serious subject and was able to fit in an internship or two during my summers. I'd pursued football fiercely, but I wasn't starting from *zero* in this other dream either. I'd had the forethought to plant the early seeds for a plan B. Or so I thought.

I scoured LinkedIn and job boards for investment banker positions, applying to anything I could find. I followed up with emails, deciphering the formula for each company's accounts from whatever evidence I dug up across the Internet. That first month and a half, I must have sent five hundred emails—no exaggeration. I went so far down the list of investment banks that it quickly turned to unrecognizable names with microscopic footprints. Still, I applied.

My two years of gaming with Kev in my dorm room returned

to haunt me. The vast majority of companies didn't even reply. Those that did only did so as a courtesy to let me know that they had received my application, but my qualifications wouldn't earn me an interview. The "qualifications" they spoke about were my GPA, which sagged well below the target range of any respectable firm, and my internships, which were in an entirely different discipline within finance. My explanation—that when I accepted the internships at big-name banks, I didn't know there were differences between the departments within a bank—didn't seem to satisfy many hiring managers.

I seldom even tried to explain the GPA that hung around my neck like an albatross. I saw the requirement, "3.5 GPA in finance, accounting, or related fields," before submitting my applications, but chose to cross my fingers and apply anyway. Through five years at Wake, the only threshold I focused on was 2.3—that was the minimum GPA needed to retain athletic eligibility. By that standard, the 2.7 I walked away with looked like a gold star. I blamed everyone around me. Why hadn't anyone told me that good grades lead to good jobs?

After weeks of rejection, I fell into an even deeper funk. Pivoting away from plan A was difficult enough. Realizing that plan B was just as much of a pipe dream would be too difficult to bear.

In the moment when I'd reached my lowest, I received a message from Eric Ramsey asking if I had time to catch up. Eric had played baseball at Wake Forest and the two of us had been friendly, though not super close. Most of our interactions were shouted over the loud soundtrack of a party in progress; I'd spot his shock of red hair and make a beeline to catch up before continuing on with the festivities. He always had an uplifting presence, though, and I was happy to hear from him.

The afternoon of our call, I heard back from the last of the hiring managers I had reached out to. No luck. I'd exhausted every option. I'd put a happy face on my disappointment ever since graduation, but now that months had passed without a whiff of progress, I just didn't have the energy. When Eric asked how I was doing, I responded with verbal vomit that captured all my shame, disappointment, and exasperation in a single run-on sentence. Then I inhaled deeply and waited to hear his bewildered response.

Instead, Eric came back at me with a simple suggestion. "You should talk to my dad. He might be able to help."

It couldn't hurt. What else did I have to do? The next afternoon I was on the phone with Mr. Ramsey, giving him the slightly more composed, but vastly more extended, version of the rant that I had delivered to his son. We went back and forth on my many goals and aspirations and how far I'd fallen short. We talked about the stakes of my decisions, all I wanted for my mom and brother. Mr. Ramsey countered with his own career path, the steep climbs and sudden dips that delivered him to a corner office. Our lives couldn't have been more different, but his, he assured me, was no cakewalk either.

Mr. Ramsey wasn't soft-spoken or tender, but I found his

bluntness deeply comforting. He told me investment banking wasn't where I belonged, but there were other careers worth chasing. He delivered the truth as he saw it: in the arc of a lifetime, the last several months would be a blip; there was still plenty of time for redemption. Keep trying. He inflated my lowly spirits.

Before hanging up, Mr. Ramsey snuck in a final word of reassurance: "Don't worry, Matt. We'll find you a job."

I would soon discover that when Mr. Ramsey said "we," he meant it. I wasn't alone in my corner anymore; this was a team effort. Before the end of the week, I had calls set with three of Mr. Ramsey's connections. All three would fall through, but each enjoyed our conversation and passed me on to a few of their friends they thought might be able to help. The cycle repeated itself as I connected with an ever-widening circle of middle-aged bankers. Rejection came just as often as it had when I was cold emailing, but it wore a kinder face now. I wasn't groping around in the dark any longer. For the first time since high school football, I felt I had a map and a destination; getting there was only a matter of time.

Finally, as I passed the six-month mark, the time arrived. Someone along the string of connections that started with Mr. Ramsey told me that his counterpart would be in Raleigh in two days on business. He told me I could meet with the man and see where things went. The conversation went well, and he invited me to attend a final-round interview at the company's headquarters in Pittsburgh. I accepted before he got the sentence out.

On the day of the interview, I looked like a bum. I didn't have a business-appropriate piece of clothing in my closet. I strode to PNC Bank's headquarters in the same clothes I'd once worn to church in high school—I was swimming in my shirt and my slacks fit like sweatpants. Adrenaline coursed through my body at a pace I hadn't felt since my last gameday.

I interviewed for a corporate and institutional banking analyst role. It wasn't the sexy world of investment banking, but it would give me the foothold in finance that I wanted. It would also provide the salary and ticket out of Raleigh that I desperately needed.

When it was my turn, I sat in the hot seat to field the recruiter's fastball questions. I flew through the technical portion—thanks to many sleepless nights, I'd wrapped my head around all the knowledge I needed to execute the job. But then the hard part started. I gave him an honest pitch. No, I didn't excel as a student. No, I didn't intern in the most ideal positions. No, I didn't have accounting or finance on my diploma.

What I did have was an unmatched work ethic and a desire to learn. I also, at present, had nothing to lose. I would work myself raw and become a standout in his firm if for no other reason than because I didn't ever want to go back home.

I flew back to Raleigh and waited seven excruciating days before hearing back from the recruiter. I landed the role. My time in Raleigh was over.

I hadn't felt such speechless joy since Coach Tindal called me with my first scholarship offer. Until then, my hopes for a corporate life had been merely theoretical. PNC's offer confirmed that yes, I did have what it took to make it in the real world; I could aspire to something beyond the football field. It gifted me a new life and the potential for redefinition.

The role included a signing bonus. Once I signed the necessary paperwork, the company deposited $10,000 into my account. I don't think I'd ever seen a comma on my bank statement before. I stood straighter after that blessing.

All told, I spent less than one year of life back in Raleigh temping—not the end of the world. But it's impossible to see the outer edges of purgatory from the center. In the moment, I had every reason to believe I might never be able to leave again.

One month later, I packed my car up with all I owned—two large duffel bags of clothes and a few pictures—and drove to Pittsburgh. Mom rode with me, and we bobbed our heads to oldies streaming out of the Beats pill as we made our way north. I didn't have a place to live when I arrived, so we cruised around the city with my life in the trunk, inspecting places I found on Craigslist. By late afternoon, I found the house I'd call home—a big bedroom in a dicey part of town that would cost me five hundred dollars a month. It wasn't the most impressive setup, but it was mine and I loved it.

No sooner had we made it to my new home, my car broke down...again. All I could do was laugh. Things could be much worse. We could be stranded in the West Virginia mountains. Or we could have not left Raleigh in the first place.

I wasn't fully out of the woods yet. The road to fulfillment would be a long one, and I still had miles to go. But, arriving in Pittsburgh, I felt as though the worst was behind me. Adulthood could commence. I'd gone up against the hardships of my old life and won.

The multi-month interlude in Raleigh underscored the importance of keeping the faith while striving for something better. Goals rarely manifest when you tell them to. I can't claim to have remained optimistic throughout the process, but I never got pushed into inaction. I kept looking for openings, kept pressing for paths out, no matter how unlikely. Knock on doors long enough, and one will open. Never let past failure prevent you from future attempts.

I also learned that opportunity must be searched for and cultivated. It never appeared with the blinking lights and name tag like I thought it might. Instead, it appeared as a chance phone call with a one-time acquaintance and the passing mention of a father whom I should consult. From there, it was a trail of breadcrumbs—one call leading to another and a string of letdowns along the way. At any point, I could have easily given up. I could have avoided Eric, or never called his father, or not followed up on the long series of conversations that followed him. Given how few prospects I had, it's easy to imagine another world in which I was too discouraged to act at all. I don't know where life would have delivered me in that other world, but I'm sure it is a place far from where I landed in this one.

You have to search for serendipity. And when you sense even the faintest glimmer of it, act. Don't wait.

> You have to search for serendipity. And when you sense even the faintest glimmer of it, act. Don't wait.

CHAPTER 8

Strive, Strive, Strive

Hold on to your dreams of a better life and
stay committed to striving to realize it.
—Earl G. Graves Sr.

Forget anything else you might've heard; Pittsburgh is paradise. I felt in awe when I first laid eyes on its sliver of a skyline, wedged between two broad rivers. With the exception of brief getaways on friends' family's vacations, and weekend trips to visit my guys, I'd spent my entire life to that point in North Carolina. I'd never lived on my own. I'd never lived in a true city. Pittsburgh captured possibility in concrete, glass, and steel.

My first days in Pittsburgh were like my first days at Wake Forest. Unlike the last time I was the new kid, I didn't have a team to slot into this time. I didn't know a soul in the entire city, but I didn't mind the solitude. I was new to adult life. I needed time to learn to ride without the training wheels. A buzzing social life would have added more to my plate than I could handle.

Instead, I learned to navigate the mundane. I befriended a nearby mechanic and got him to look at my clunky beast. I joined a local gym. I strolled about my new home, working to get my bearings amid the concrete forest.

On weekends, I rose early to get to the courts before the games started. I played pickup basketball for hours each Saturday—it's not like I had anything better to do—and slowly, I met friends. I became a familiar face to the other regulars at the court and gravitated to like-minded guys. You can tell a lot about a man from a game of pickup. His vanity, honor, and work ethic are laid bare on the court. I befriended a few men early on who have stayed with me to this day.

I'd never had two pennies to rub together, so I was used to living on little. Even though PNC paid me a decent salary, I refused to change my lifestyle. I saved all I could, making a game out of watching the small number in my account grow. I bought a big loaf of multigrain bread each Sunday and turned it into my lunch for the week ahead. I spread chunky peanut butter on one side and drizzled honey on the other and stuck two of those sandwiches in the break room fridge. Dinner would be a pound of pasta. With the money I saved, I splurged on flights to Houston or Baltimore. Not having to vibrate down the highway in my lemon was luxury enough for me.

During the week, life was simple. Rise early, work hard, sleep little, do it again. The home I found was just down the street from the bus stop that took me straight to the office door. In the winter months, the sun was still shaking off sleep when I took my seat on the bus for the ride. I had an underdog mentality about my work with the company. Though I felt I belonged, I knew I was there in part by the grace of others. Few with my résumé would ever have been allowed to claim a spot among our ranks. I had something to prove. I arrived well before others and went home after they finished, staying to study the concepts I hadn't yet mastered once my work was done for the day. I wouldn't make my hiring managers regret their decision.

Soon, others around the firm took notice. I was hard to miss in the first place—there weren't many other six-foot-five-inch Black men walking around our hallways. But the hours I put in and the work I produced attracted attention. Co-workers stopped by my desk more often, leaning over to discuss last night's game or this weekend's plans. They invited me to drinks after work, where I felt more comfortable sharing another side of myself that they didn't know. I spoke about my former NFL dreams and the magnitude of the PNC opportunity in my eyes. Unbeknownst to me, word started to spread that one of the new analysts had gotten a tryout with a few teams. And that's when the emails started coming in.

"Hey, Matt, heard you're quite the athlete. We have a company basketball team and would love to see you come out for it. Games on Thursday. Hope to see you then." I looked at the email signature. I recognized it from the dozens of training videos I was still working my way through. A senior executive at the bank was reaching out. He ran one of the departments I was set to rotate through in a few months. How did he even know my name?

In the days that followed, I seldom left my desk to cross the office without hearing words of encouragement from strangers. They stopped me in the hall—"See you on Thursday, right?" with a wink and a nod, or "I was so happy to hear you decided to join our team" with a pat on the shoulder. They rarely introduced themselves, assuming, I'm sure, that I'd been around long enough to know who they were. When I got back to my desk, I'd ask the other analysts who I'd just spoken to. "Oh, that's the head of so-and-so" or "the vice president of such-and-such." Leadership took company basketball remarkably seriously and, in a funny way, I felt like a high school recruit all over again.

Sports did more for my corporate career than I ever imagined it would. Roaming the office, I came across serious men who stalked the hallways in a flurry of pinstripes and warm cologne. Those same men could be found on the court after work, throwing themselves to the ground for a jump ball. On the sidelines, they loosened up. I saw another side of them beyond the professional façade they displayed during work hours. In me, they got a workhorse. They saw how I worked on the court and extrapolated it to my performance in the office. They respected my hustle. It was a blessing for me, a no-name analyst new to town. I literally rubbed shoulders with management.

Basketball gave me a way into an office culture that would have otherwise been foreign to me. Leadership embraced me now, high-fiving as we passed in the hallways. They scouted me for other teams too. On my way out of the building one evening, I received an email asking if I'd join the run club.

I showed up to a local park three days later and recognized the first man I saw. His was the first face I saw when I opened my laptop in the darkened office each morning. He was my screensaver. He rocked side-to-side in a power stance, running cap, running shorts, shirtless and absolutely shredded. Bill Demchak, CEO of PNC. Next to him stood the CFO, stretching and talking shop. The chief security officer, whom I recognized from the many lessons on cyber-security, did high knees off to one side. The company basketball team had managers, but running club was of a different order. This was an elite group, comprised of only the highest-ranking senior leadership and employees who had also led at Division I cross-country programs. We did seven miles together after work. Some people ran at a six-minute pace. Some ran quicker. No one wanted to be in the back of the pack; we gritted our teeth and muscled through the streets.

While we warmed up and cooled down, I grew close to Bill. He wore these odd-looking, chunky-soled shoes that lifted him two inches off the ground. Tired of seeing me show up in the same tattered Nikes run after run, he gifted me a pair of his platform runners—the same pair I'd later wear on my first marathon.

Seeing Bill and the other executives up close, it was obvious why they'd been so successful. Their drive verged on insanity. Here was a man who led one of America's largest financial institutions—a twenty-four–seven endeavor—and ran Olympic-distance triathlons in his spare time. The same could be said of all the C-suite executives I ran alongside. They achieved excellence because they saw no other option—they demanded it of themselves. I recognized that commitment; they approached every side of life with the same intensity that Kev and Mike brought to football. I felt privileged to see that mentality at work up close. I modeled my drive in their image.

One year in, life in Pittsburgh was everything I hoped for and more. I filled into adulthood well. I excelled at work and had the ear of the bosses who could shepherd me to success. I even formed a small posse in the city, which meant leaving less and enjoying home more. Then a single trip turned my world upside down.

Pat Long and I had lived together for two years in college. He was a year behind me and a couple of inches shorter, but sure of himself and athletic; a splotchy beard strayed across his face, and his hair stood to one side like he'd styled it in a wind tunnel. He was from Jersey and member of a Northeastern class of old money and prestige that I didn't know existed until I got to college. Junior year, he traveled home for Princeton University's homecoming, and I tagged along. He showed me the difference between Raleigh rich and Ivy League rich—there were levels to this shit. After college, he moved to New York, as did most of the Northeasterners we knew. One year into my Pittsburgh experiment, he invited me to come visit him in the big city. "It's a quick trip from Pittsburgh. You'll love it."

The Greyhound bus from Pittsburgh to New York was a redeye—I boarded at eleven p.m. Friday and rode through the night, fast asleep for the hours-long journey. I awoke with the warm glow of sunlight peeking through my eyelids and eased myself upright. As my sleep daze wore away, new confusion set in. What was this place? Outside of the window, concrete mountains erupted from the pavement and dueled in the sky. I couldn't see the tops of the buildings from my seat in the bus window, which made sense— judging from their roots, they were never-ending. And the people! They spilled out from every crevice, zigzagged, then returned. They melted to a seascape of bobbing heads in every imaginable color. This wasn't Pittsburgh. This was the thing that ate Pittsburgh.

The bus came to a stop at seven a.m., and I shot off like a bullet from a chamber. I had to breathe in this relentless mass of humanity.

Pat's place was on the Upper West Side, twenty-five blocks from where I stood. I walked through each of them in amazement, more than eager to discover what lay around each corner.

I stepped into Pat's apartment and immediately understood the complaints I'd heard about New York rent. Pat paid some multiple of my rent for a shoebox. It was an endearing shoebox—two small bedrooms and an even smaller living room with a futon that I'd call home—but a shoebox nonetheless. Pat and I hugged hello. "You want to rest?" he asked. Absolutely not. So much city was happening outside, and I was missing it all.

My days in New York went something like this: walk to Pat's CrossFit gym and work out. Work harder than Pat to prove I still got it. Go home, shower, eat—a true New York–style bagel, both fluffy and dense, better than any I've had. Central Park calls. Stroll around, take in the view, meet friends, exchange numbers. We're late to the bar now! Pass on the cab because I'd rather bike instead. Look up in wonder like they do in the movies as we pass Times Square. Arrive at the bar but park far away so we can walk the last few blocks. Buy a round. Gasp at the bill. Say cheers, then go again. We're going to miss our reservation for dinner. Treat myself; I deserve it. Order the steak. Eat a better meal than Pittsburgh can muster. Close my eyes and inhale.

I had barely seen Gucci Shane since our night at High Point a few years before, but I remembered that he told me he lived in New York now. I promised I'd hit him up if I ever made it out his way.

The sun had set on the city by the time we stepped out of the restaurant, but you wouldn't have known it from the sounds on the street. I got a whiff of a second wind. The city was just getting started.

I said bye to Pat and left to search the city for Gucci. I arrived at the address he sent me and doubted seriously that I was in the right place. Again, I looked up; the mound of glass disappeared in the night sky.

The elevator collected me from the lobby and deposited me on a mountaintop. Gucci Shane's mountaintop. I stepped straight from the elevator into his living room, which is apparently a thing in New York City penthouses. Who knew?

Gucci Shane showed me a whole other side of the city that I hadn't yet explored. A mass of people floated around his apartment in dark leather and high heels. The men wore matching gold watches. They played beer pong on marble countertops and paired plastic cups with expensive liquor. Gucci Shane called this event a pregame, which made my imagination spiral over what the game must be like.

I didn't have to wait to find out. The game was a nightclub. Tables and bottle service and more people in leather. Going out with Gucci Shane was like going out for Super Bowl weekend, only these were regular kids, balling like athletes. Laughing, and joking, and running up tabs I couldn't fathom. We split a ten-dollar pizza at the end of the night, during a sliver of time that could have just as easily been called morning.

Pat and I had planned on another early morning workout, so I stopped by his place to change then ran right over to the gym with him. It had been twenty-four hours since I'd last slept, yet adrenaline pushed me onward. Another New York day followed, more sightseeing and delicious meals. I boarded a redeye Greyhound back to Pittsburgh near midnight, forty sleepless hours later. I got home just in time for a quick shower before work.

On the ride home, when I should have been too exhausted to open my eyes, my mind raced. I revisited all the conversations I'd had over the past two days. All those people were so sure of themselves. They spoke of their ambitions like they were destinations instead of dreams—failure hadn't even occurred to many of them as a distant possibility. They were masters of their own universes.

I returned to my life, but I couldn't unsee New York. Pittsburgh, a city I had adored only days earlier, seemed lifeless now. The energy that pulsed through New York was too magnetic to ignore. Within days, I was clamoring to return. Whatever I wanted for my life, I knew my path would have to lead through that big city.

I sent out feelers for positions in New York that same week. At Gucci Shane's pregame, I'd met Jamie, who saw the wonderment in my eyes and pounced on me about moving to the city. "I'll connect you with my HR department if that's what it takes." He did just that. The role at his company wasn't a great fit, but they offered to connect me with other organizations.

The new role was at a digital media startup, a left-leaning

millennial news outlet that premised its entire business model on deriding Trump. I interviewed to be a media planner. I didn't know the first thing about media, planning, or media planning but I knew the position was New York–based, so it checked all my boxes. The company put me through the wringer—fifteen interviews with people at every rung of the organizational ladder. They called each of my references, dialing people from the PNC sphere that I trusted would have something good to say. Finally, I got a call from the CEO. The position was mine if I wanted it. I accepted before we hung up.

The choice was a bit crazy. Pittsburgh and PNC had both been great to me. I'd discovered new friendships to cherish and had unfettered access to leadership at my company. More than that, Pittsburgh had been the site of my growth from boy to man. The city held a special place in my heart for that reason alone.

New York almost certainly wouldn't nurture me as Pittsburgh had. The city was many things, but it wasn't coddling. My income would drop, and my expenses would skyrocket—I wasn't getting a bedroom of the same size anywhere on the island of Manhattan.

But perhaps that was the point. In a year and a half in Pittsburgh, I proved that I could thrive in a place that moved faster than Raleigh. I expanded my comfort zone and tamed a city that once appeared as an unruly challenge. It was time to become uncomfortable again.

I timidly tiptoed into my boss's office when it was time to

announce my departure. He had supervised me since I first arrived, and our bond ran deeper than professional ties. I started to tell him that I was moving on, but I choked up before I could get the words out. I was closing a monumental chapter of my life. He stammered through the conversation breathily. The emotion surprised us both.

When I arrived back at my desk, an email waited for me. It was Bill Demchak's assistant, summoning me to his office that afternoon.

He cut to the chase. "Tom tells me you're leaving. Why?" For ten minutes, I explained my lust for New York and my new media planner role. I recounted a (somewhat edited) version of my weekend in New York and my newfound love for the city. He sat, stonefaced and attentive. I watched the thoughts pace through his mind. Then he said, "Look, Matt, we're prepared to do what it takes to keep you, so what do you want?" He saw the confusion on my face and explained, "If you want to transfer to the New York office, I'm happy to make that happen. If you want exposure to another part of the bank, pick a department. You are an asset to us. I can't watch you go."

Of the many ways I thought the conversation might go, I never predicted a blanket offer to stay. Now, it was my turn for silence. I considered the offer, how wonderful it would be to embark on this new adventure while staying close to the familiarity I loved, treading into deep water with a lifeline attached.

But didn't that defeat the purpose? Yes. This next stage was about growth. Familiarity wasn't a friend. I needed to stretch myself again.

I thanked Bill for his generous offer but told him that I needed to move on. He nodded that he understood and wished me success in whatever came next.

Before moving, I sold nearly everything I owned. I wouldn't need the clunker car or the few pieces of furniture I'd collected where I was going. Plus, I needed the cash. I had created a small cushion during my time at PNC, but New York could squander that in no time. All that remained were two plastic storage bins that I squished my whole life into.

Like my move to Pittsburgh, I arrived in New York without a clear idea of where I'd live. Unlike my move to Pittsburgh, that problem was not quickly fixed. Rent was a serious problem. I discovered just how severely Pittsburgh real estate had spoiled me. The measly five hundred dollars I paid for my old room wouldn't get me a closet in New York. I reached out to Pat before moving and he offered me his futon until I got on my feet. I doubt either of us realized then just how long "getting on my feet" would take.

Pat still lived in the same small apartment that I visited. It was a studio apartment that he and his roommate had partitioned with a temporary wall. On one side was a small bedroom where Pat's roommate, Connor, slept. On the other, a dual living room/bedroom where Pat slept, just large enough to squeeze a double bed and a futon. The futon would be mine. Our understanding was that I'd camp temporarily while apartment hunting. When all was said and done, my temporary stay had turned into three months.

From the first night I arrived in the city, my new life began, and with it, the strained adjustment to New York living. First, there were the expenses. I entered New York thinking that I could live frugally, just as I had in Pittsburgh. Why change my peanut-butter-and-pasta diet when it was working for me?

Frugality and New York City don't mix. It's hard to leave home for less than twenty dollars. And I left home a lot. That was adjustment number two. I sprinted through my first three months in the city the same way I had my weekend-long visit. I can't honestly recall a night during that entire period when I slept more than four hours. I turned into a "yes" man. Club on a Tuesday? Yes. Brunch on Sunday? Yes. Happy hour on Thursday? See you there. I felt like I'd missed out on so much, spending my life in North Carolina and Pittsburgh. I tried to make up for twenty-five years of lost time in a few months. I got home in the a.m. hours most nights. And I loved every second of it.

The final adjustment, and most difficult to grapple with as time went on, was sacrificing every shred of personal space. I was so grateful to Pat for giving me a place to rest my head. But, not wanting to impose, I was always hyper-aware that I lived in someone else's living room. I tried to make myself small, being scarce when they had company and never having company of my own. I got home after they went to sleep and left before they rose, and I snuck around, mouse-like, in the few hours we overlapped. What little time I did save for rest wasn't particularly restful.

None of the growing pains tinted my rose-colored view of New York. Beyond the pure electricity of it, I fell in love with the diversity of the place. New York was as close to a meritocracy as I'd ever encountered—much more so, certainly, than Raleigh. Work your ass off in this city, you'd be rewarded for your efforts. I saw more women and people of color in positions of power during my first week in New York than I had in a lifetime in Raleigh. That's not to say the institutions I encountered in New York were perfect, or even generally equitable, but they were leaps and bounds ahead of what I'd grown up with. I couldn't imagine the white men I knew back home ever reporting to someone who didn't look like them. I didn't realize how I'd taken that truth for granted until I moved to New York and saw that other realities were possible. The success of many others energized me.

After three months with Pat and Connor, I needed to move on. The two had been supremely generous, but it was time to strike out on my own. I found an open room on Craigslist that was only a few blocks away. I could have it at $760 a month for two months. I shuffled my few pairs of jeans and button-downs back into the plastic bins I traveled with and carried them over to my new home.

Unknowingly, when I left Pat's, I commenced a new, eventful, and above all else, strange phase. A search for living space in New

York on a tight budget will take you on a tour of the oddest corners of the city.

Apartment #1
Codename: Kitty Kamikaze
Location: Upper West Side
Roommates: 2
Cost: $760/month

I had two roommates in my new apartment—one young, one old. At twenty-six, I landed somewhere between Jackson, an undergrad, and Larry, an octogenarian. The move-in interview presented all sorts of red flags—Jackson couldn't make it, so Larry fixed an old-school camcorder inches from my face and recorded my responses to a long list of unrelated, invasive questions. I didn't care. I had picked the place off Craigslist because it had a room I could call my own. I was desperate. He offered me the place after laying down a slew of arbitrary rules I needed to follow. I ignored every one of them and agreed.

On move-in day, Larry re-emphasized Rule Number One: No closed doors. His cat, he said, suffered from anxiety. Closed doors only made it worse. "Whatever," I thought. I stacked my stuff into my new home, thankful for the space.

My first night in the apartment and first in months in a room of my own, I closed the door, flicked on the TV, and soaked in the isolation. I've always slept to the sound of the TV. My thoughts get too loud otherwise. I'd just begun to slip away when…

BANG!

A slap rocked the door and startled me out of my cloudy sleep. I jumped over to the door and poked my head out; Jackson and Larry were tucked away for the night, and the tiny living room sat dark and empty. I considered that I'd imagined the noise. After weeks of living noisily, maybe my mind played tricks on me. I closed the door behind me but hadn't made it back to my bed when…*BANG!* Another loud shock jolted me to attention. When I opened the door this time, I saw Larry's cat at my foot, stumbling dizzily.

This time, I stepped out of the room and closed the door behind me. I sat on the couch facing my door, hoping to catch the ghost knocker. I watched as Larry's cat shook himself awake and stumbled uneasily over to the kitchen. Then, apparently no longer in a daze, it turned and shot off at a full sprint toward my room. Once it got even with the couch, it took flight. The cat launched itself several feet away from the door, a feline missile cutting through the air. It crashed into the base of the door with a crack and crumpled to the ground. And then, as I sat there, the cat picked itself up, dusted itself off, and stumbled drunkenly back to the kitchen for another round.

From then on, I left the door open.

Not a week later, I was back in my room, asleep while the TV watched over me. I'm a light sleeper and have, on occasion, been accused of sleeping with my eyes open. I can neither confirm nor deny whether that is the case. Anyway…through my hazy vision I saw the shadowy outline of a man. He stepped forth from the dark living room and up to the foot of my bed, within the TV's glow. In a single, swift motion, I rocketed out of sleep and into a fighting stance on top of my mattress. When my eyes adjusted, I saw Jackson: skinny, pale, and in nothing but his tighty-whities. He held the remote in his hand.

"You can't have the TV on if you're going to leave the door open. I can't sleep."

One month down. That's it. I got to get out of here.

Apartment #2
Codename: Flea Market
Location: Midtown East
Roommates: 1
Cost: $1,000/month

I found the next apartment just as I had the last—on Craigslist. I agreed without even looking at the place—anything would be an improvement on my current situation.

I stepped into George's apartment and noticed instantly that he'd failed to mention a few things on his Craigslist ad. First, George was a hoarder. Standing at the front door, it was near impossible to see the floor, except for a thin path that ran the length of the apartment. Walk that path, and be surrounded on all sides by old magazines, torn-up denim, and broken Crock-Pots. Second, I didn't have a room, I had a rectangle. George had cordoned off a six-foot-by-eight-foot section in a corner of the living room for my living space, just large enough to fit a twin mattress and my plastic bins. I got no privacy. I heard every sneeze, snort, and fart that came out of George, and there were many. Finally, there were cats. I think George had four in total, but no one could say for sure. Fortunately, they weren't anxious, but that was probably because they had so many friends to commiserate with. When it was time to shower, I walked across the apartment and felt the kitty litter sticking to the soles of my feet. I washed off with the dribble of his shower head, then played the "the floor is lava" on my way back to my cell, hoping to stay litter-less long enough to slip my shoes back on.

Two months in. Enough already. Time to move again.

Apartment #3
Codename: Puff, Puff, Pass Out
Location: Midtown
Roommates: 2
Cost: $800/month

I found the next apartment off of...you guessed it...Craigslist. This one was a one-bedroom. It didn't allow pets; I checked. The owner, whose name I don't know to this very day, took the bedroom and never left it. I truly mean *never*. He kept his door locked, and I didn't see him the entire time I lived there. The occasional cough or hiccup was all that told me he was still alive.

In the living room, he inflated two air mattresses, set them side by side, and rented them to strangers for $800 each. I took one. Vinny took the other. Vinny worked as a kitchenhand in a restaurant somewhere in Midtown, so his sleep schedule was just as off-kilter as mine was. Vinny had a touch of crazy to him that I might not have minded in an acquaintance, but because we slept inches away from each other, it made me fear for my life.

Vinny also smoked. A lot. All day and all night, smoke streamed out of his nostrils like a forest fire burned in his lungs. We shared a small apartment, so stepping into our shared living room/bedroom was like swimming into a cloud. The scent clung to me; I couldn't wash it out of my skin, hair, or clothes. I grew paranoid about the stench I felt following me into each room and sitting beside me. At work one afternoon, I coughed and tasted the sour tobacco tang in the back of my throat. That was the last straw. It was time to pack up again.

Throughout all these many housing mishaps, my work product suffered. I was chronically sleep-deprived. The thrill of life in New York, combined with the drawbacks of time at home, meant that I spent every waking moment roaming the city. After dozing off in a board meeting, I was given a warning and placed on a performance plan. I was lucky not to be fired. I'd gone to crazy lengths to save money in the city. I finally realized that the hundreds saved wouldn't be worth much if they got me fired from my job.

My exhaustion aside, I struggled to stay engaged with the new job as the weeks wore on. I was thankful to the company for bringing me to New York, but it soon became clear that I was not meant to be a media planner. The work just didn't interest me, and it lacked the sexy, fast-paced rhythm of life at a big bank.

In my weaker moments, I wondered why I had ever plunged into New York in the first place. I had built a great life for myself in Pittsburgh, one marked by stability and a clear path to the promised land. What sane person leaves all that for crazy cats and cigarettes?

But every time I left my apartment and reentered the zany maze of Manhattan's streets, I remembered my reason. Making it in this city would mean seeing all of my dreams, even the ones I hadn't had the courage to conjure yet, come true.

While I ping-ponged between strange dwellings, Pat had escaped the city. A new project sent him to Los Angeles for six months. I flew to visit him one weekend when I simply couldn't take the aroma of tobacco any longer.

It was my first time ever visiting California, and the sunshine felt rejuvenating. I spent time with Pat and his new girlfriend, who was from LA. They kindly invited us to her family's home for dinner one night. I'd been deliriously tired for so long that I was just happy to downshift and eat a home-cooked meal. At dinner, her father regaled us with nostalgic stories of his heyday in New York.

I shared my love for the city and my disappointment with work. He told me he worked at a commercial real estate company called CBRE and that he could make some calls. I'd never heard of the company, but judging only by his fifteen-foot ceilings and crystal chandeliers, I assumed it was a big one.

I jumped on the opportunity once I was back in the city. Within a month of the trip, I'd interviewed three times, including twice at the company's headquarters in the iconic MetLife Building, hovering above Grand Central station. Yes, this was a big one. I pounced on the offer they extended and submitted my resignation to the news outlet the next day. My days as a media planner were over.

With my new salary, I could finally spring for a year-long lease in the city. My first place was a 550-square-foot, three-bedroom apartment. It was tiny and crowded, but it was mine. I'd pick the roommates this time.

When I arrived in the apartment for the first time, I collapsed onto my bed and slept for fourteen hours straight. Over the next month, I didn't go out once. I didn't realize the toll that living in limbo had taken on me. I just slept. Night after night. I emerged a month later as though for the first time. Seeing New York through rested eyes was like watching a brand-new city fall from the sky and land upon the old one. My love for the place deepened further.

With my new job and apartment, things would only continue to improve over the next year. Once again, I had stepped into the wilderness of uncertainty and emerged on the other side better off.

Now, on the other side of that uncertainty, I think about how easy it would have been to remain in Pittsburgh and avoid adversity altogether. I have nothing but fond memories from my time in that city. To this day, I am in touch with former co-workers from PNC, young professionals who started on the lowest rung like I did. Those who stayed are in management positions now and, given our age, deep in wedding planning and baby showers. They live wonderful lives—lives that could so easily have been mine.

But when reflecting, I think also about how much happier I am now, having learned to overcome frustration, stress, and self-doubt. What CBRE offered, in terms of my own happiness and interest in the work, was well beyond anything I could have hoped for at PNC. New York was the right call. I had to release one life before I could grab hold of another, the one I was meant to lead.

Contentment is bliss; we should all strive to find satisfaction in the world we organize around ourselves. But complacency doesn't complement contentment; it distances us from it. Had I stayed in Pittsburgh, I'm sure I could have built a beautiful life, but the unanswered questions of whether I could have handled New York would have lingered. Over time, they would have eaten away at me.

As we grow, our goals must adjust, elevating to accommodate our improved view of the world. I believe deeply in listening to your ambition when it tells you to move on. Sometimes growth requires taking two steps back to leap ten steps forward. In the midst of that step-back, progress begins to look a lot like loss. In those moments when doubt creeps in, it is important to remember your reason for taking a risk in the first place. If the decision was well considered and committed to fully, then the only thing left to do is have faith in the process. Growth is uncomfortable. If you feel out of place, then you're on your way.

> Growth is uncomfortable. If you feel out of place, then you're on your way.

CHAPTER 9

Purpose Feeds Your Soul

*Passion is energy. Feel the power that
comes from focusing on what excites you.*
—Oprah Winfrey

I rolled through my New York life breathlessly for two years, but slowly, my infatuation with the city faded. I still loved the fast pace of the place, the constant buzz that coursed through its streets, but the halo I'd placed above it began to dim. I was still a North Carolina Southern boy, and despite the allure of this new adventure, a piece of my heart was left behind in Raleigh. I missed home.

The same went for that sexy new real estate job of mine. My first job at CBRE was as a researcher, not yet trusted to be a full-fledged broker. The role meant late nights and early mornings, paying my dues in any way I could. I worked alongside viciously intelligent people who, like me, dreamed ambitious dreams and worked tirelessly to achieve them. It was grunt work, but if I stayed the course, I'd soon have a big job at a big firm.

The job was everything I'd worked so hard for, ever since I pivoted away from my NFL dreams. And yet, success didn't taste as sweet as I'd hoped or expected it would. It is a strange feeling to work your ass off for a single goal, only to get there and realize that it isn't all that you expected.

Football, banking, real estate—my goals changed over the years, but my attitude toward them never did. All my life, I had tunnel vision for my aspirations. I trained to be singular in my purpose; like so many young people, I understood that as the only path to brighter circumstances for myself and my family. Suddenly, I was without a goal to chase. That, plus the routine of New York—the monotony of it

> Football, banking, real estate—my goals changed over the years, but my attitude toward them never did.

and its general loneliness—left me longing for more. I was missing something, but I didn't quite know what it was.

On my first trip to New York, back when I was still living in

Pittsburgh, I connected with Gucci Shane. I hadn't seen or spoken to Shane since that party at High Point nearly four years earlier, but I didn't know a soul in the city and figured he might have a few recommendations to share. Characteristically Shane, he went above and beyond to make me feel at home. When I suggested that we grab dinner, Shane said he knew just the place: Bobwhite. He spent all week hyping it up, but I was skeptical. Shane's a foodie and he knows his stuff, but I love to eat, and I know my stuff too.

I never should have doubted Gucci Shane. Bobwhite lived up to the hype. It's a Southern restaurant in lower Manhattan that serves up as delicious a plate of soul food as any I've ever had in North Carolina.

Once I moved to New York, I became a regular. When I felt low, Bobwhite was a refuge from the relentless pace of the city. Two times per week or more, I'd rent a Citi Bike from my neighborhood in the Upper West Side and pedal the nearly five miles to Bobwhite. I started going for the flavors of home—mac and cheese, collards, and fried chicken that crackled with each crunch. But soon I was returning for the atmosphere, the homelike friendliness that I missed. Each time I stepped inside, the fry cooks and servers rang my name out in a chorus, slapping five and holding fists out for bumps. Finally, a place where I felt fully myself in this vast and unconquerable city.

After lunch one afternoon, I stepped out of the restaurant to find a crowd of kids gathered around on the corner by the bike rack.

I spent a moment observing before strolling over. My chest swelled with nostalgia. There were six or seven boys, and each looked no older than twelve. You could see their individual tastes just coming into bloom—colorful hoodies, tall tees with graphics splashed across the front, Nikes with the laces tucked. They reminded me of my old AAU teammates, the way they filled the sky with laughter, taking turns ragging on each other.

Just like the AAU days, when I finally did step up, I quickly became the butt of the joke. "Aye, aye, look! Dude looks like Frozone!" They all doubled over with cackling belly laughs. A skinny kid off to the right chimed in, "Nah, nah, look, y'all—he look like the Black dude from *Criminal Minds*!" The howls grew louder. My pants were next. I was wearing high-waters. They had a field day.

I couldn't let them do me like that. I still knew how to play this game. I got one for his glasses and another for his jagged hairline. Their original surprised expressions quickly twisted into smiles. Soon we were all shaking with laughter.

Another one spoke up. "You don't look like you from here. Where you from, Frozone?"

I told them the Upper West Side, but they looked confused. "Oh, I've never been there. What's it like?"

Now it was my turn to look confused. Sure, it was a long bike ride, but my neighborhood was only a few stops away on the subway. I painted a picture of it for them—quiet and right on the water, nice but borderline elderly at times.

"That's cool. But what you doing down here?"

I pointed across the street to the reason why I'd come: Bob-white, the best soul food in all of Manhattan. Only place to get affordable Southern food this far down the island. How lucky were they to live right up against such a storied institution?

The group shrugged back. "Never been," they said in unison. I laughed, assuming this too was a joke. "Nope," they said, "never tried it."

Crazy, but surely they'd tried Miss Lily's, just up the block, or Dos Toros, two streets over. The group looked at me like I'd spoken in Russian. I listed all the places I knew in the neighborhood, *their* neighborhood. They'd never heard of any of them, despite living only a couple hundred steps away.

They told me what they ate instead. Ramen, McDonald's, whatever came. They listed processed food and junk from the bodega. A couple of the kids skipped meals when they had to; they didn't have consistent homes to return to and thus struggled to eat regularly. They'd never sat at a restaurant and on a daily basis ate junk food that would only worsen their health outcomes.

I felt disappointed to know that they lived right at the seat of so much opportunity and experience yet hadn't been exposed to any of it.

Before we said our goodbyes, I asked them what school they went to. They told me PS 188, the neighborhood school. We shook hands and went off our separate ways.

The encounter with those kids stuck with me all through that night. At work the next day, I looked up PS 188. I learned that nearly half of the students there were homeless—one of the highest rates of student homelessness in the city. I felt ashamed for my earlier surprise that they hadn't been to the neighborhood food spots. Sure, *I* thought they were affordable, but affordable is relative; they couldn't be within reach for students who rarely knew where their next meal was going to come from.

I Googled a map of that area and dropped pins at all the different locations that likely contained new experiences for the kids of PS 188. Luke's Lobster, Tompkins Square Bagels, Speedy Romeo. Before I knew it, I was on the phone (this was not one of my most productive days as a real estate broker). I called each restaurant around the Lower East Side with a simple proposition: let me come in with a few dozen kids one afternoon to show them all that their neighborhood has to offer. I reiterated my encounter from the day before when I had to and explained that these kids were from the nearby projects but had never been exposed to the flavors of their community. I wasn't asking for a handout; I offered to pay for the meals myself. In every case, the response was enthusiastic. Feeding kids was a mission that every restaurant

> I felt disappointed to know that they lived right at the seat of so much opportunity and experience yet hadn't been exposed to any of it.

was excited to get behind. Only one problem remained: finding kids to feed.

I emailed the principal of PS 188 out of the blue, which, looking back, was never a winning tactic. I laugh now imagining what she must have thought of that first note to her: "Hey, my name's Matt. I'm a grown-ass man that met some of your students on a corner outside of a restaurant. Mind if I take them to lunch?" I'm sure she thought I was a nut. She didn't respond.

A week dragged by, and I couldn't get the idea off my mind. I checked my in-box every ten minutes—nothing. Fed up one afternoon, I decided to just show up and hope for the best.

The only thing worse than "grown man emails asking to take kids to lunch" is "grown man walks into school asking to take kids to lunch." This too was a less-than-perfect idea, but what other choice did I have? I hurried over to PS 188 during my lunch break and walked right up to the principal's office. The door read "Ms. Ramos" and just as I went to knock, her assistant, Ms. Esther, interrupted. "Excuse me, what do you think you're doing?" I told her I was there to see Ms. Ramos; I had an idea I had to discuss with her.

"That's not how this works. Ms. Ramos is tied up in meetings until late this afternoon."

"Oh, that's no problem," I responded. "I can wait." The woman looked at me in disbelief. She explained that it would be hours before Ms. Ramos was freed up. "Sounds good, I'll sit right there." I pointed to an uncomfortable-looking chair in the corner.

Two hours later, I had my audience with the principal of PS 188. Ms. Ramos was kind but stern. She told me about her nickname—the beggar principal—which she earned by going around town asking anyone who'd listen to provide for her community of students. She gave me a tour around the hundred-year-old institution. As we walked, she pointed to kids and shared details about their home lives. She shared stories of trauma and displacement that are still difficult for me to reflect on. By the fourth child, I cut her short. "You're not going to scare me off, Ms. Ramos. I'm serious about this." Her eyes scanned my frame up and down, taking the measure of me. After a long moment, she seemed satisfied. "All right then, let's do it."

I chose to call this new experiment of ours "ABC Food Tours," a nod to the part of Manhattan it originated in—Alphabet City—but also a reference to "getting back to basics." I wanted to build tours that focused on education at least as much as nutrition, leaving kids with a firmer understanding of the fundamentals of healthy eating and an active lifestyle.

Within weeks, we were off on our first food tour. I didn't have to think long about where we should make our first stop; Bobwhite was the obvious choice. One sunny afternoon, I returned to the restaurant I knew best with Ms. Ramos and twenty-two young ones in tow, feeding them the chicken and biscuits I'd grown to love. They smacked their lips and scarfed them down just as I had on my first visit. From Bobwhite, we went to Speedy Romeo for a demonstration of wood-fired pizza. Then we were off to Pause Cafe around the corner to sample Moroccan dishes. The list of stops for that first trip was six restaurants long, but the children spent so long marveling at the pizza process that the sun was already dipping low in the sky. Pause would have to be our last stop. Next time, I'd know to leave plenty of time for wonder.

Even before returning the kids to school, my mind was already racing with improvements for our next tour. I got back to my apartment that evening feeling reenergized and grateful. Before bed, I shot off emails to schedule the next trip.

Soon, ABC Food Tours was off to the races. On weekdays throughout the year, I picked up new groups of students and showed them around their own community. What started with nutrition exclusively quickly expanded to a more holistic view of health and wellness. We took yoga and meditation classes together. We went on long jogs and scrambled through obstacle courses. And, of course, we ate. A lot.

Those initial months of the program were not without their own challenges, though. It didn't take long for me to understand why Ms. Ramos had insisted I understand the community she served before making any grand promises about what I could do for them. All sorts of difficulties cropped up that I couldn't possibly have anticipated.

Our single greatest hurdle was attendance. It was simply

impossible to predict how many kids would show up for any given food tour.

One particularly disappointing example comes to mind. Over a year since the first ABC food tour, we'd really hit our stride. We'd expanded beyond PS 188 and offered tours to schools across Manhattan and Brooklyn. We'd built relationships with dozens of restaurants across the two boroughs as well, but there was one that had been on my wish list from the start that we couldn't quite nail down: Bowery Meat Company. This is one of the best steakhouses in New York, and I knew our students would get a kick out of its old-school feel. After appearing on *Rachael Ray*, we were granted the opportunity to partner with them. We picked a Friday, and they set aside forty-five meals to share with the students. I'd looked forward to every food tour with anticipation, but Bowery Meat Company was a league apart. I couldn't wait for our kids to explore the inner workings of such a storied institution.

On the day of the Bowery Meat Company tour, three kids showed up.

The start time arrived, then drifted by, and we waited. Gradually it became clear that no one else was coming. I must admit, after denial, embarrassment was the first emotion that rushed me. So many months of schmoozing and logistical headaches invested in this day, and it would not be at all how I described. I wondered whether the steakhouse would ever be willing to work with us again.

After embarrassment came the more significant heap of disappointment. I tried to hide it away, but I doubt I succeeded. I wanted so badly to share the magic of Bowery Meat Company with kids from the community and to watch their awestruck faces beam. However, we would press forward with the tour with the three kids who had come, but I wished it could have been more. Maybe I was wrong to think that ABC was having any impact at all.

Days later, Ms. Ramos explained the truth of the situation to me. Then she told me to get over it. At least ten of the kids didn't come to school that day. Another five had family issues that interfered. Two more had moved back to Colombia just in the time since signing up. Ms. Ramos told me that on any given day, right up until the last day of the school year, she could expect to welcome a small handful of new students into her school and to learn that a few others had left—such was the nature of working with a community where nearly all of the members lived below the poverty line and almost half were homeless.

The conversation with Ms. Ramos granted me much-needed perspective. The kids we served had dealt with a greater number of real-world problems in their short time on Earth than many would in their entire lifetimes. Of course they couldn't all make it—they had plenty else to deal with. The discussion helped me to redefine success for ABC Food Tours. Of course, I wanted to impact the lives of as many kids as possible, but that was ultimately beyond my control. What I could control was the way I invested in every student who came along for a tour. That would have to be the new goal—to center each one and to recognize each as an individual. To make him or her feel both seen and heard. With the chaos that swirled around so many of their home lives, parents who dealt with stresses beyond imagination, it was on me to ensure that, while the students were on a food tour, they felt like the world was theirs.

This subtle but significant shift in mindset allowed me to find the small victories in every tour we embarked on. The organization continued to grow, and reach was still important, but just as important were the personal connections with students that enabled them to unload the weight they'd been carrying. Jayden's was one such story.

I met Jayden during ABC's second year in operation. With more than a year under our belt, we'd scaled our tours to include dozens of schools across the city and felt we really had the hang of things. Jayden was a third grader from another Alphabet City school but was the size of a middle schooler. We had taken every other grade from Jayden's school on tours at that point, and his was the last, so the kids were eager to join in the fun from the moment we announced they'd be next. Not Jayden, though. Experience had

> The organization continued to grow, and reach was still important, but just as important were the personal connections with students that enabled them to unload the weight they'd been carrying.

taught me to tune in closely to how the students interacted with one another and the advisors at the start of each new tour. Early in the day, I knew Jayden was one to keep an eye on.

The day we'd planned was one for the record books. We had an all-star list of restaurants to visit: Miss Lily's, Luke's Lobster, Bob-white, and Tompkins Square Bagels—all my favorite local spots. Miss Lily's—an authentic Jamaican restaurant nearby—was the first stop.

Everything at Miss Lily's is delicious, but the fruit punch was the star of the show for the kids that afternoon. The staff at Miss Lily's couldn't mix it quickly enough; gallons disappeared as soon as they hit the table, sending the chefs right back to the bar to mix more pineapple and guava. Jayden was loud in his approval, guzzling it down and licking a ruby-red mustache onto his upper lip like everyone else. But he turned his nose up at the food, not even daring to touch the jerk chicken and sweet plantains we brought out.

Luke's Lobster was next up. Luke's had become a regular part-ner of ABC Food Tours. I appreciated the group's commitment to sustainable sourcing and the father-son pairing that brought the brand to life. More than that, though, I loved that they enabled us to expose our students to lobster, a food they'd long heard of but never tried. In many of their minds, lobster was synonymous with luxury. At Luke's, we showed them that this mythical food—and the life they associated with it—was within reach.

During every trip to Luke's Lobster, we had to overcome the hurdle of unfamiliarity. When the first batch of crab and lobster rolls appeared, a chorus of *ewwww*s and *what's that*s invariably erupted. It took a lot of coaxing and, at times, ice cream bribery, to get the students past their hesitation, but we always got there. By the end, they were usually calling out for seconds.

Jayden, again, was the exception. Whereas he turned up his nose at the Jamaican food, at Luke's he announced his disgust proudly. He drank the juice again, but he refused to go anywhere near the lobster rolls and teased the kids who chose differently. Some of the other students began to follow his lead, choosing not to engage with the activities we'd laid out for them. We were eventually able to move past the disruption and onto a fun and productive event, but Jayden never ate a single bite.

Third stop of the day was Bobwhite. Given how Jayden had reacted to the last two restaurants, I looked forward to introducing him to the Southern flavors I adored. Fried chicken and mac and cheese? What's not to love? Bobwhite was always the stop that students went home talking about later in the day. Its soul food could put a smile on even the most stubborn of faces.

As always, I perked up at the smell of fresh baked biscuits and still-sizzling chicken. All the students did too, chirping up with *ooh*s and *aah*s. The staff had prepared for our arrival and laid out biscuit bottoms and chicken thighs for the students to assemble their own sandwiches while hearing about the journey of the restaurant's founders. Kids giggled, spreading biscuit crumbs across their laps and sucking on their honey-stuck fingers.

Here, too, Jayden was unimpressed, refusing to indulge in even a single bite.

But everyone loves chicken biscuits! This was the final straw. What more could I do to break through to him? His disruptions had been a drag to the experience that other students were having. What was up with this kid?

I pulled Jayden aside to check in. "Hey, buddy, what's going on? You haven't eaten a single thing all day." After an entire afternoon of outbursts, Jayden quieted now. His eyes dropped to the floor and his fingers grew fidgety.

"I just don't like this stuff, that's all," he said just above a whisper.

"Oh, I know that can't be true, those chicken biscuits are something else! Come on, man. Tell me what's up."

Jayden continued to stare at the ground for a moment longer; then, seeing I wouldn't let it go, he slowly reached his sweaty palm into his right pocket and produced a to-go cup of banana pudding from Miss Lily's. "My sister has always wanted to try this stuff, so I thought I'd take some back to her." Then he reached into his left pocket and pulled out a lobster roll, soggy and nearly dripping. "And my mom has always wanted to try lobster, so I'd feel bad if I tried it before she did."

"But why not just join in, Jayden? Everyone is trying new things together. We want you to ask questions and engage with our hosts. Why you acting like you don't want any of the food?"

His voice quieted even further. He was barely whispering now. "I can't eat today."

I looked at him, puzzled. What? Why?

"It's my birthday..." He paused and looked up for the first time since we'd begun speaking. Nervous tears welled in his eyes. "...and my mom has been saving up to take me to Chipotle for a special dinner, so I have to stay hungry until then."

What could I say? I felt a lump come together in my throat and choke me up. I'd spent all day thinking I had a problem child on my hands, that Jayden hated the tour we'd brought him on and acted out as a result. I couldn't have been more wrong—he cherished the experience so much that he spent all his energy figuring out how to take it home with him.

I looked down at the food still clenched in his sweaty palms. We'd tramped across the East Village in ninety-degree heat for a full afternoon. The food had nearly turned to mush, yet he clutched it like a trophy he'd won.

Jayden told me how much his mom had looked forward to treating them to Chipotle that day and how important it was to him that they share it together. I heard in his tone the strain of a boy just trying to do right by his mother and felt the love he had for her. Of course, it brought back memories of when I was that same boy.

Moments and conversations like that made all the effort worth it. I considered how Jayden, at only eight or nine years old, had chosen to sacrifice in order to bring a smile to his family's face. I wondered how he'd learned the importance of responsibility and duty so early. When I say that the students of ABC Food Tours taught me far more than I ever taught them, I am thinking of students like Jayden, who, even as a child, had developed greater strength of character than many adults I knew. I felt overwhelmed with pride and sadness simultaneously—pride that we'd fostered an environment where Jayden could share his truth and sadness that he'd had the carelessness of youth snatched away from him at such a young age.

When we finished speaking, Jayden rejoined the group and didn't have another outburst all day. He engaged with the restaurant owners, asking insightful questions, and laughed along with his peers. He nibbled here and there, but still didn't indulge the way the others did, and I didn't press him to either—I understood how important it was that he hold on to his appetite.

Before the tour ended, while the students were deep into the last activity of the day, I checked in to make sure the staff had things under control then dashed out the door. I revisited every stop we'd made and left with to-go containers stuffed with the day's fare. Before saying goodbye to the students that day, I thanked Jayden for hanging out with us and handed him the boxes—soggy pocket banana pudding was no way to enjoy dessert.

We gave tours to students hailing from every borough. I was invited to speak before the annual convention of the New York City Elementary School Principals Association. The message I delivered that day was one of empathy for the kids who overcome such long odds to show up prepared to learn each day. But also hope, having seen how far a little investment could go in inspiring the kids I worked with.

I was proud to see ABC Food Tours gaining recognition after the several years of work we'd poured into it. We had established ourselves, no longer having to beg and claw our way into every new partnership. But still, time with the students was my greatest reward. Looking back, no acknowledgment or accolade could have compared to the experience one student's mother gifted me after we included Rafael, her son, on a food tour.

Rafael was an absolute star. He came to the tour excited and stayed engaged all day, enthusiastically diving into the new foods and asking questions that made even the experienced entrepreneurs pause to consider their answers. In the post-tour debrief with Ms. Ramos, I raved about the kid I'd watched shine. I asked her how I could empower him further; he had so much potential inside of him.

Ms. Ramos called Rafael a model student then offered to connect me with his family. Later that afternoon, I stood before his mom, the matriarch of a seven-member clan that included Rafael, his four siblings, and her close friend, who had been shacking up with the family for months. Rafael served as translator for his mother while she raved in Spanish about the experience her son had had that day. She insisted that I come to her home for dinner the following week so that she could thank me properly.

On the day of the visit, I brought along my friend Javier to serve as both translator and cameraman, capturing what I knew would be a rich experience. I offered to buy the groceries for the meal, making clear that we were happy to stock their fridge, covering anything she added to the cart. At checkout, the total came to twenty dollars. Despite our prodding, she refused to include anything she didn't absolutely need for the night's meal.

Rafael's family lived in a three-bedroom apartment, but only one of the rooms was theirs to use. The other two were accorded to two more families, both nearly as large as Rafael's. I saw the room they shared but didn't step inside; doing so would have meant standing on someone's bed. The entire floor was covered corner-to-corner in tattered mattresses that served as the shared resting place for a family of seven.

Stepping into the family's unit, I considered what a miracle it was that Rafael had become such a standout. I didn't see a desk in the whole unit. Siblings buzzed in and out of rooms, leaving no hope of privacy or quiet. How did he focus on schoolwork with so much action all around him?

When it was time to cook, everyone had their marching orders. Little ones rolled the flour and set the table while his mom sliced chorizo and stewed the beans. They used every shred from the groceries we'd purchased, down to the very last black bean. She served the table and we dug into a meal that was totally delicious. She turned twenty dollars into a meal for nine.

While we ate, Rafael's mother spoke about the family's journey from Mexico to America. She told of how they fled in the middle of the night to escape her abusive husband, Rafael's father. Javier didn't have to translate when conversation turned to her arrival in America; I saw the glow of gratitude for a nation that granted her safety. Javier recorded our discussions around the table but always kept Rafael's aunt just out of frame—she'd escaped her own abusive history and didn't yet feel out of its long reach.

In Rafael's home I felt a concentrated dose of the same emotions ABC Food Tours had given me all along—empathy, gratitude, and an overwhelming respect for the strength of the human spirit. I can't quite describe how special it felt that they saw fit to bring me into their home and feed me, but I thanked God that night for bringing me to their doorstep.

ABC Food Tours lifted me out of the drudgery of my New York day-to-day and pointed me back toward my purpose. It brought me full circle, merging the many phases of my life—Raleigh, Wake Forest, New York—in a way that once didn't seem possible. In the time I spent with the kids of PS 188, and eventually, kids from schools across the city, I recalled the days when I was in their shoes—young, Black, and dealt a hard hand, but hoping for something better. I felt reenergized after my time with those students. Our time together encouraged them to aspire to greater heights. What could be more meaningful than that sort of impact?

For years, my ambition had propelled me along my professional path, first toward the NFL, then into corporate life. As long as I could remember, I'd wanted most desperately to provide for my family the luxuries that we could never afford in my childhood. But after settling into New York, I felt myself slipping into a rut. I felt unfulfilled at work, and detachment seeped into the other areas of my life. ABC Food Tours was the reset I needed. Ambition alone wasn't enough. Purpose made life worth living.

Few are quick to find meaning in their work, to find their purpose. I was blessed to have stumbled upon mine that day in Alphabet City. If you're in search of yours and unsure of where to begin, my advice is simple: start with acts of service. For me, there's nothing quite so animating as seeing that a long day's work had a direct impact on the lives of others. And if you try it and it's not for you, at least you left the world a little better off along the way.

> Ambition alone wasn't enough. Purpose made life worth living.

CHAPTER 10

When in Doubt, Say Yes

Do not fear mistakes. There are none.
—Miles Davis

I was never meant to be the Bachelor, and not just because of the unlikely odds that a Black guy from Raleigh, North Carolina, must overcome to lead America's favorite franchise. I mean I *really* wasn't meant to be the Bachelor—the furthest step I ever planned to take into Bachelor Nation was as a contestant on *The Bachelorette*. And even that much was a stretch. But 2020 had twists in store that no one could have predicted.

My Bachelor story begins before ABC announced my selection, even before *The Bachelorette* producers first came calling. The seeds for my acceptance were planted in mid-2019, when Tyler Cameron, my roommate and closest friend, returned from his own *Bachelorette* journey.

Tyler and I had stayed close since playing football together at Wake Forest. When I moved from Pittsburgh to New York in the summer of 2018, Tyler made a similar migration from Florida into my apartment on the Upper West Side. He became one of my first roommates after the era of apartment musical chairs ended. The two of us folded ourselves into a two-bedroom shoebox with bunk beds, bean bags, and room for little else.

Tyler was the first to take the Bachelor plunge. We hadn't lived in New York together long before he left for a month of filming for Hannah Brown's season. When he returned to our apartment in New York, we tried to resurrect normalcy from our hectic lives, but things had changed. He had newfound fame and an unresolved relationship to contend with. The season aired and controversies, big and small, claimed front pages on dozens of tabloids. Seemingly everyone had an opinion on Tyler's romance, who he should and shouldn't settle with. I had a front-row seat for the transformation, and I noticed how things changed in our day-to-day routine— turning heads followed us now to the restaurants and hangouts we used to slip into anonymously.

For my own part, I juggled my job at CBRE, which had ramped

up while Tyler was away, and the burgeoning ABC Food Tours, which had become a huge commitment. With any downtime that remained, I rode with Tyler to events and appearances around the city, shaking hands with the people who comprised his new world. Soon, this new crowd became familiar, and it greeted me with the same warm smiles and hugs that it heaped upon him.

Producers for *The Bachelorette* were a big part of this new universe. Tyler's commitments to the show extended well beyond the After the Rose ceremony, and several times per week we rode the length of Manhattan to connect with the behind-the-scenes characters who brought the show to life. Before long, they turned to me curiously: would I ever consider joining the franchise?

My answer was simple: no.

Things were looking up, and I had plenty on my plate at that point. Tyler and I had just moved into a new apartment that rose high above the clouds and seemed plucked from a dream of mine— bye-bye, bunk beds. At CBRE, I was on track to become a full-fledged broker and earn the uncapped commissions the role promised. I couldn't just step away from the office for weeks on end after working for years to get to that promising point in my career. Plus, who would run ABC Food Tours in my absence?

> Before long, they turned to me curiously: would I ever consider joining the franchise? My answer was simple: no.

The producers persisted. They weren't outright pushy, but each time I ran into one of them while out on the town, a coy grin spread across his or her face before asking me whether I'd reconsidered. For months, my response remained the same—I hadn't. I truly had no interest in straying from the path I'd laid out for myself. Only someone with remarkable powers of persuasion could shake me off my stubborn stance. Ms. Cameron was that person.

Just as I'd grown close to Tyler over the years, I'd also fallen into his family's fold. His mother was the matriarch and a pillar, not just for her three boys, but for their entire Jupiter, Florida, community. She clung to me like a fourth son and always made me feel welcome while on my summertime visits to their hometown. Besides her warmth, she also had a no-nonsense core, hardened over years of raising a houseful of boys; she shared her wisdom whether you asked for it or not.

For Thanksgiving, we welcomed the whole Cameron clan to our new apartment to celebrate the holiday. While the brothers caught up, I lent a hand to Ms. Cameron, cheffing up a feast in the kitchen. In between directives, she put on a businesslike voice. "Tyler told me that they're trying to recruit you for *The Bachelorette*." From her tone alone, I could tell where she landed on the issue, but I laid out my many counterpoints anyway. What of CBRE, ABC Food Tours, and the aspirational life coming together before me? I had just taken a risk in leaving my role in Pittsburgh to come to New York. Was now really the time to press my luck?

Ms. Cameron let me finish, and when I had, her reply was characteristically straight: "You're making a mistake."

Ms. Cameron pressed me to reframe my thinking. Set aside the professional tradeoffs, she insisted, and consider more deeply the opportunity for personal growth. She'd seen changes in her son since he returned from the show. A few were apparent even to me—his emboldened confidence and refined communication skills. But she spoke of deeper shifts. She saw how the process forced him to confront the past struggles that he'd long hid from. He examined his own discomfort with past relationships and reconsidered their role in his life going forward. Then she turned her attention to the struggles she knew to be nagging at me, just below the surface. Many years into adulthood, and I hadn't yet explored what it meant to be in love. "Opportunity doesn't always come when you're ready for it. You need to face your challenges head-on, Matt. I want that for you."

As the conversation drifted into increasingly uncomfortable waters, I felt my guard rising. I relented. Fine. She wanted me to submit a video, I would submit a video. Then I stuck a thermometer in the turkey and asked how much longer she thought it should roast.

I'd almost forgotten about our conversation three days

> "Opportunity doesn't always come when you're ready for it. You need to face your challenges head-on, Matt..."

later, when I got the first of many reminder texts from Ms. Cameron. Had I submitted my video yet? No, but I would. Try as I might, I couldn't drag my feet on this forever. One slow evening, I sat in front of my webcam and explained why I thought the *Bachelorette* experience could be meaningful for me. Then I shut my laptop and, having satisfied Ms. Cameron's hopes, expected to close this chapter entirely.

Two days passed, and an email appeared in my in-box. The producers would be in New York that week; would I consider coming to the offices to meet them? I was still hesitant but, like the video itself, this too seemed like a harmless formality. Soon enough, they would find a reason to toss me from the process, and I could move on with life.

After that first meeting, there were others. More in Manhattan. More still over the phone. Some producers I'd met before. Many I hadn't. All the while I stayed honed in on the brokerage business, coming up for a conversation at the producers' request, then resubmerging myself into the work at hand, paying little mind to the process outside of the few minutes a week I spent with its architects. All the while, Ms. Cameron stayed attuned to my progress. I didn't tell anyone else I was going through it—not even Mom—seeing no point in raising hopes over nothing. But when Ms. Cameron called, I assured her I was sticking with it.

Christmas was near when I received an unexpected call asking if I'd like to fly out to Los Angeles to meet with the remaining members of the team. There was a disorienting heft to their invitation that I hadn't felt before, as though I'd sleepwalked for the journey and awoken only to arrive at my destination. This, I knew, would be the last step to secure a spot on the upcoming season. To get on that plane to California would be to accept everything that might come after. I lost sleep mulling over what it might mean to divert my path again, when I'd only just settled into my new life. In the opening days of 2020 and for only the second time ever, I boarded a flight to Los Angeles.

The "interview" that followed, if you can even call it that, was all fun. I explored LA's neighborhoods, relishing a break from the bleak East Coast winter and inhaling the ocean air. I spent afternoons with producers fielding their many questions on my past and future. Why are you single? What is your type? Have you ever been in love? Why not? I answered everything as directly as I could. If I was going to do this thing, I would enter as the real me. On the flight home, I had no idea whether I would be getting a call back, but I felt grateful for the experience nonetheless.

In the weeks that followed, two phone calls pushed my emotions into opposite extremes. ABC rang first. I'd passed the process and they wanted to formally offer me a spot in the upcoming season of *The Bachelorette*. I thought myself in circles for days and had made my mind up well before the offer came. I accepted. I didn't yet know who the star of the show would be, but I was excited to embrace the mere possibility of love.

I had to get my affairs in order. I had to notify CBRE of my upcoming absence, and I had to buy a new wardrobe that followed the series' strict guidelines. I had to field early interview requests and I had to read up on the experience ahead of me. I had to attend to the detailed minutiae that comes with leaving home for several weeks on end. After that, there were "goodbye-for-now" dinners and lunches, time spent with loved ones ahead of our short stint apart. I'd just settled it all when I received the second call, which nearly crushed me.

I instinctively knew something was wrong when I saw Tyler's name appear on my caller ID. Tyler and I text often and FaceTime occasionally, but we never speak on the phone. He spoke in sharp, curt statements. "Something's come up. I'm on my way to the airport. I have to run down to Jupiter for a few days. I'll catch you up later." I knew not to press for answers. I could hear his voice straining as he spoke. Moments later, another friend rang to fill me in. Ms. Cameron had had a brain aneurysm and was in critical condition. Her prognosis looked grim.

For three tortured days, I looked to the journey ahead of me and reflected on Ms. Cameron's guidance, which had delivered me to its doorstep. I recalled our last Thanksgiving together and the many conversations since, when she pressed me to embrace adventure and discomfort. I reached out to Tyler and offered what I could, but what could I really do for him, an eldest son in an impossible situation? On the fourth day, Ms. Cameron passed on.

I flew to Florida to celebrate the fifty-five remarkable years that Ms. Cameron had graced this earth. I packed two big trunks—I wouldn't be coming back to New York for a while. In Jupiter, I saw firsthand the beauty of her life, as few friends and many strangers spoke of the astounding impact she'd had in their community. We cried often. But just as often, we laughed, trading nostalgia over the memories she left us with. I stayed in the family home for a few days after her celebration of life. I fit in where I could, helping with the many logistics involved with burying a loved one, but also, in private moments early in the morning or between errands, checking in on my close friend and brother. And then, when my time was up, Tyler drove me to the Palm Beach airport, and I boarded a plane bound for Los Angeles.

The untimely loss of Ms. Cameron was an ominous foreshadowing for the often difficult, always unpredictable year that followed.

First, the pandemic struck. I'd already traveled to Los Angeles and was waiting for filming to begin when a producer knocked on my door and told me to pack my bags. Production had been shut down. We were to go home and return in three weeks, when things would be up and running again. Even under normal circumstances, entering a *Bachelor* production is like entering a bubble—we sacrifice our cell phones and lose all contact with the outside world. Once production halted and my phone was returned to me, I called Tyler in a state of bewilderment. He told me New York City was shutting down and it was time to get out. "Don't fly back there.

Meet me in Jupiter." I followed his directions and flew back to where I'd just come from.

I, of course, did not return to Los Angeles three weeks later as planned. COVID-19 spiraled into a global catastrophe and, amid the fear and uncertainty, filming, like most other activities, paused indefinitely. I was bummed, of course, feeling as though I'd jumped through countless hoops only to be denied the opportunity that all my effort had led to. But I didn't dwell on it. The world faced chaos. On the list of global concerns, one delayed season of *The Bachelorette* was far from the top.

I returned to a home in mourning. A few weeks since Ms. Cameron's passing, and the initial shock and fray had settled. The family was left to grapple with the reality of continuing on without her. Oddly, the global pandemic presented a welcome distraction, despite its dark overtones.

I wasn't the only escapee seeking refuge at the Cameron home. Friends from across the country descended upon Jupiter to bunk up for however long it might take for the storm to pass. It felt like summer camp. I've always been an early riser. At Camp Cameron, strolling to the kitchen in the morning required tiptoeing over and around the bodies strewn across the house. Every soft surface became a bed. During the day, we pranked, ran, laughed, sailed, stretched, and danced our way through sluggish summer afternoons. At night, we Netflixed, gossiped, and played cards. We made our lemonade from sour circumstances.

Someone had the idea to name this new group of ours the #QuarantineCrew, and soon we were posting videos of our antics across social media, garnering more followers and views than any of us could have anticipated. The new following breathed life and purpose into our daily activities. We partnered with major charities, repurposed for COVID relief efforts. We created branded content and donated the proceeds to frontline workers' funds and the Robin Hood Fund which, like ABC Food Tours, assisted underserved kids in New York. It wasn't just about fun anymore. Or distraction. Or coping. We were trying to make a difference.

Soon as our new platform took root, another shoe dropped. Back in March, two days before Ms. Cameron's passing, ABC had announced its latest *Bachelorette* star—Clare Crawley. An alumna of several *Bachelor* franchise seasons, Clare was a familiar face to Bachelor Nation, but an utter stranger to me. I'd never watched a single episode of the series except for bits and pieces of Tyler's edition, so I didn't know anything about Clare other than what was covered on her *Good Morning America* segment. I intentionally didn't look any further into her background before leaving for Los Angeles. I liked it that way. I felt strongly that, for love to stand a chance to grow, we both deserved to begin with a clean slate.

But it was my off-camera life that proved problematic. Clare had seen our TikToks and called me out publicly for chasing fame in the run-up to her season. Without listing me by name, she tweeted about those who were "creating Cameo accounts before you are even on my season…you are in it for the wrong reasons…#dontwasteyourtime," clearly a reference to a recent appearance I'd made with good friend and New York Giants' wide receiver Alex Bachman to benefit the Robin Hood Foundation. The sentiment backfired. On Twitter, Bachelor Nation quickly pounced, rushing to point out the worthy cause our work benefited. I appreciated their support, but it was hard to take any positives away from the tiff. I hadn't met Clare, yet I still held out hope that, once the world was back up and running, there might be chemistry for us to discover. As her comments traveled across blogs and tabloids, it felt like our potential romance would collapse before it had even begun.

The temporary filming interlude stretched past a month, and then even longer, and soon I doubted that I'd ever return. The producers went radio silent for weeks at a time. I threw myself into the day-to-day goofiness of life with the crew. I began looking for new jobs back in New York. *The Bachelorette* just wasn't meant to be.

Then Derek Chauvin murdered George Floyd and suddenly, everything else mattered less. I've already described the anguish I felt in that moment. The confusion. And the conversations I had in its wake. It was overwhelming and isolating.

I felt thankful to have Tyler by my side then. Ms. Cameron had fostered a home that was welcoming to people of all stripes, and she raised her boys to be as unprejudiced as anyone I've ever known. Tyler grew up in diverse environments and thus had never been timid about engaging in difficult conversations on race. He seemed as bothered by what he saw on that video as I was. The two of us protested together and visited local community leaders to discuss what more could be done. Bachelor Nation is a group that skews toward conservatism. I hadn't even appeared on a season, but the announcement of me as a contestant put me on viewers' radars. Perhaps I could get through to this group in a way that many Black leaders could not. What was my burgeoning platform for if not to effect change in this precise moment?

Separate from my efforts, the reverberations of Floyd's murder quickly reached the corporate offices over at ABC. In forty seasons across *The Bachelor* and *The Bachelorette* franchises, there'd only ever been one Black lead. I didn't grow up with the series and was unaware of the underlying diversity issues that had long plagued it. But unbeknownst to me, during closed-door meetings among ABC executives, I was beginning to look to them like a solution.

I received a call from a Los Angeles number randomly, after weeks without contact. The man on the other end claimed to be a producer for *The Bachelor*. Not *The Bachelorette*. *The Bachelor*. We made pandemic small talk. He asked how I was faring with the Clare Crawley fiasco. Then out of nowhere: "So, what do you think about being the Bachelor instead?"

How did this troll get my number? If it wasn't someone in the house pranking me, then it was a fan with too much time on his hands. Either way, I was uninterested. I knew firsthand how the vetting processes for these series were structured. There were months of interviews, phone calls, and check-ins—people didn't just call out of the blue offering up a season lead.

My first thought, after considering that it might be one of my friends, was that someone was trying to catch me off-guard, a cheap attempt to sell magazines. I was still in the midst of the Clare Crawley controversy, being accused of joining the series for all of the wrong reasons. The many people who rushed to my defense understood that clout-chasing wasn't my thing, that all my public efforts had been for worthy causes. But what if the tabloids got a recording of me considering becoming the Bachelor? The headlines would write themselves: "JAMES, EAGER TO BE A STAR, GETS WHAT HE WANTED ALL ALONG."

"Nope, I'm good, man." Nobody was going to make a fool out of me. The producer asked if I was sure, I told him yes, and then we hung up the phone and that was that.

Twenty minutes passed by and the *what-ifs* began to taint my firm resolve. No one texted to say they'd almost had me. I wasn't tagged in any rogue recordings on Twitter. It was a long shot, nearly impossible really, but what if I'd just turned down the biggest opportunity of my life without giving it a second thought? Thankfully, the phone rang once more. It was the producer again. This time there was no small talk, just two words: "You sure?"

For a brief moment, I remembered Ms. Cameron again. I remembered her urging me to chase after opportunities even, or perhaps especially, when I didn't know where they would lead. I considered the rush I felt after accepting the role with *The Bachelorette*, the thrill of opening myself up, for the first time, to the possibility of falling in love. There was a vulnerability to that choice, exposing myself to the world, defenseless, that felt foreign. Becoming a season lead would elevate that feeling to the tenth degree. There would be responsibilities and missteps and embarrassments. But there would be growth as well. And, if I was lucky, I might even find a woman to spend my life with.

I didn't hesitate. "I'll do it."

"Okay," he said. "We'll set up a call for Saturday. In the meantime, don't tell anyone—not your mother, not Tyler, no one. Talk to you soon." And just like that, I accepted the role that would change my life.

The following Saturday, I spoke with the lead producers who would shepherd me through the chaotic process ahead. Gone were the touchy-feely questions that landed me the *Bachelorette* role. These conversations were all tactical. There were studio execs to meet and trainings to undergo. There was a whole vocabulary to learn (*We have Bachelor Nation, Matt, not fans*). Did I have an agent? How about a publicist? Well, I would need both, stat.

The lead producers set a time for the big announcement, only days away. I would have an entire segment on *Good Morning America* devoted to my upcoming season. Before then, they would block off a full day to run me through the *Bachelor* crash course. I'd meet the entire team top-to-bottom and receive the rulebook for leading a *Bachelor* franchise.

Few people know this, but even at that point, when I should have rolled downhill into my own season of *The Bachelor*, I *still* nearly managed to lose the role. I was still in Florida with the crew of friends who had shacked up at the Camerons' home. The producers set the date of my crash course in all things *The Bachelor* for the same day that Tyler had chartered a boat to take our group fishing. It wasn't a problem; we were set to depart in the morning, while all the producers on the West Coast would still be asleep. We'd motor out, cast our lines, and haul dinner back to shore that afternoon, leaving plenty of time for me to change and hop on Zoom. The Floridians among us were experienced boaters, but I'd never gone out on a charter before and felt excited to tag along.

We boarded in the morning hours, shaking hands with Captain Bobby, our guide for the day. I sat in the rear of the boat as he sped off, watching the dock shrink smaller and smaller before vanishing altogether. The sun blanketed my body, and I dozed to the calm lull of the ocean. I shook awake when the captain called out that it was time to drop our lines. I shot my head up and scanned 360 degrees around the boat, orienting myself. There wasn't any land in sight. I checked my watch—I needed to be back on shore in two hours to make the first call, and I knew we were already nearly that far away from home. "Hey, Captain, I'm not sure if I mentioned this already, but I have a few meetings to get to today, so if you could just shoot me back over to shore when you get a chance, that'd be great." Captain Bobby paused with a puzzled look on his face, and then erupted in laughter. "Oh no you don't, son. This is a fishing day! This boat isn't going anywhere until later this evening. Now, enjoy."

My heart sank. I looked around frantically for ideas, but what could be done? We were a speck in the ocean without another sign of life in sight. I checked my phone—no service. There was nothing to do but sit back and plan how I would beg for forgiveness upon my return.

When I got back to the house, I typed out emails furiously. The team didn't mask their justified disappointment. Several executives had carved time out of their busy schedules to meet with me, not to mention the rank-and-file staff who had constructed a curriculum for the day. *Good Morning America* had blocked out a whole chunk of time just for me; now America's most-watched morning show would need to find another slot because I'd gone fishing. More than embarrassing and unprofessional, the mistake threatened my continued involvement with the series.

Fortunately, the team was willing to forgive, though they made it clear that I'd used my final lifeline.

Of the many topics that arose when we finally did make time for our day-long discussion, nothing was emphasized more greatly than my race. I knew it wasn't a coincidence that the producers asked me, a Black man, to lead the franchise in the wake of George Floyd's murder. I didn't, however, know that I would be the first ever to do so. I never watched the show, so I wouldn't have known a former Bachelor if he sat next to me. If I thought about it at all, I assumed that there must have been another Black guy over the series' multi-decade run. Only after I accepted did the executive producing team mention that I was a groundbreaking choice and, given the current climate around racial injustice, a necessary one.

> I knew it wasn't a coincidence that the producers asked me, a Black man, to lead the franchise in the wake of George Floyd's murder.

Listening to the producers frame me as their new golden boy, a symbol of their progressive attitudes, I suddenly felt put off from the position. I could see myself being tokenized in their eyes. The last thing I wanted was to give the series, which (I would soon discover) had long faced allegations of discrimination, undue absolution. The conversations transported me back to elementary school, when the greatest compliment anyone seemed to have for me was that I was "different" from the other Black kids they knew. Would I be betraying my own people by stepping in to help this franchise save itself from a PR nightmare?

But then I considered what my acceptance could mean for mainstream culture. It's easy to be dismissive of *The Bachelor*, but its reach is undeniable. I considered the impact I'd have if I brought distinction and dignity to that iconic role. Millions of people would watch me, a Black man, be principled and vulnerable for weeks on end. My very existence could press white people on their prejudices or broaden the possibilities that young Black boys saw as available to them. What if I could be the example for others that I'd long wished I had?

Rather than slowing down the process, I doubled down. I wanted this now. For myself. For my family. For onlookers, eager to see themselves on one of America's biggest stages. I couldn't possibly have foreseen all that would follow that critical decision, but one thing I knew for sure: my life would never be the same.

A new Bachelor announcement provides its star a particular relationship with fame. Traditionally, fame is a slow drip. You get noticed in your hometown mall, then while out and about in the streets of a nearby city, and eventually, things snowball until your anonymity is squandered. Being announced as the Bachelor is closer to turning on a fire hose. One moment you exist in relative obscurity, and the next, camera lenses peek out from the shrubs in your yard.

The night before our grand *Good Morning America* announcement, I phoned Mom and John to check in. This was the calm before the storm; in twelve hours, the last of our anonymity would vanish. "You did this, Mom. This only happens because of how you raised your boys. I love you so much." I remembered this moment in Tyler's trajectory and remembered how the media soon hounded him. My voice dropped an octave. "We'll be honest with each other the way we always have been. Don't read any of the stuff on the Internet. You won't learn anything true there that I haven't already told you." Then, less assuredly, and as much to myself as to them, "Don't forget, we'll be the same people tomorrow that we are today. Nothing changes." All they could say in return was how proud they were of me.

There were ten of us living in the Cameron house at the time. I loved the crew, but in those final moments, I needed privacy. Grace, one of my closest friends from Wake Forest, had just arrived in Jupiter to ride out the pandemic with her boyfriend in her family's home. She offered me escape, and I accepted. The next morning, I dressed in a pink blazer, blue button-down, and swim trunks and spoke to the *Good Morning America* hosts from Grace's living room. My face was beamed into millions of homes around America. There was officially no turning back. Soon as we wrapped, I returned to my phone to check in with my family and the producers. We'd only just gone off air, but already, my phone chimed to no end. I cut it off and left it in my room.

The day that followed was utterly normal. Conspicuously so. We went out on the Camerons' boat—I ditched the blazer and was ready to go. We loafed around the house. We went for a celebratory dinner at Hog Snappers. The staff at the restaurant greeted me just as they had all week, and the swordfish sandwich tasted the same as it had the day before. It was a charade—I couldn't stay in Jupiter forever—but I clung to that normalcy before reentering a world that had, in an instant, transformed around me. When I did return, I did so as America's first Black Bachelor.

Sometimes, after years of work and prayer, opportunity presents itself in the most unpredictable of ways. If you had told me during my time as a Wake Forest Demon Deacon, or as a banking analyst, or even when 2020 began, that I would one day become the star of *The Bachelor*, I would have laughed at you. Right up until the very moment when I was offered the role, it was not even on my radar. Looking back, it is easy to impose a sense of logic onto the past as though it had been there all along; to think that where I ended up was a matter of destiny and the only possible outcome given all that preceded it. I know that isn't the case, though. There are luck and blessings to account for. For my own part, drive and resilience played a role. Just as important as all these was risk-taking; leaping into the unknown and trusting that I would land in a better place than I launched from.

Doing so requires a confidence in your own capabilities that felt foreign to me initially. It also requires a near-delusional resistance to complacency; looking at your surroundings, no matter how comfortable, and believing that you are never more than one opportunity away from elevating everything you see, then being brave enough to seize the opportunity when it arrives. I will be forever indebted to Ms. Cameron for pushing me to see the possibilities beyond what lay immediately before me. She saw a vision for my future long before I saw it myself.

When opportunity arrives, all you can do is say yes, and have faith that your life experiences have prepared you for that moment. To do anything else is to lead a life full of regret.

> When opportunity arrives, all you can do is say yes, and have faith that your life experiences have prepared you for that moment. To do anything else is to lead a life full of regret.

Epilogue

I never wanted to write a "*Bachelor* book." I haven't read *Bachelor* books, but I have assumptions about how they might read. The depths, or lack thereof, they might explore. A hyper-focus on the franchise, which they might fall victim to. I didn't want *this* to be *that*.

The Bachelor, though life-changing, was only a months-long sliver of my lifetime. I reached manhood years before our first day of filming. I traveled a long way from Raleigh to Nemacolin, and I wanted this book to tell the story of that journey—a story that went largely untold during my season. Most importantly, I wanted to share the principles that guided me along that journey. The end to my story is still an open question mark, but if I can provide guidance to others pressing through adversity, I should. And hopefully, thousands of words later, I have.

But I realize that no book of my life so far would be complete without the series that put me on the map. So, with that said, here we go. Let's talk about my season of *The Bachelor*.

The *Good Morning America* announcement kicked up a whirlwind that only expanded through the summer weeks. I thought things were intense before; they turned to madness. I frantically revisited the checklist I had ticked off before leaving for *The Bachelorette*. Everything had to be done over again with greater intention. I gave more interviews and made more appearances. I got my house in order—fielded calls from lawyers, agents, and publicists all clamoring to come aboard. I talked with ABC staff about logistics. Endless logistics. I bought more clothes! How do I pack for an entire month of appearances on national television? I needed suiting and a tux or three. By the way, how do I tie a bowtie?

All the while, COVID continued to roll through America. The death count climbed, and quarantine life in Jupiter, once a blast, stagnated. Too much of a good thing can become a drag. The environment hadn't changed, but I had. I was antsy to embark on the new adventure that awaited me at Nemacolin. I spoke with the show's producers, and they agreed it would be a good idea for me to arrive early to get acclimated to the resort that would be our set. My time in Jupiter ended in August when I flew to Pennsylvania. I had come to the Camerons' home for a two-week stay. By the time I left, it had been five months.

I landed in Pittsburgh a month and a half before filming began. A coordinator assured me a car would greet me at baggage claim.

Waiting at the curb, bags in hand, I broke out into laughter when a big-body Rolls Royce slowed to my side. This couldn't be life now. Out hopped Tim, a tall man with callused palms he'd earned from a long career as a jack-of-all-trades. I asked where we were headed next. "What do you mean? I'll take you wherever you want to go." The right answer was the Nemacolin resort—my hosts expected me soon. But I'd landed in my old home town—Pittsburgh—for the first time since moving away years earlier. I had weeks at Nemacolin ahead; what difference could a quick detour make? Tim pointed the car toward the best wings Pittsburgh had to offer, William Penn Tavern. As we drove, I peered out the window at the landmarks I once sped past. I reflected on all that had changed in the three years since I left the city. Everything. Most notably, the car—this wasn't the same Chevy Trailblazer I once rolled down Walnut Street.

Tim and I sat in silence in the restaurant, filling our mouths hand over fist with saucy wings. We only paused to talk Pittsburgh sports, Pittsburgh food, and Pittsburgh politics—anything but *The Bachelor*. He wiped his hands before steering the Rolls Royce to the resort I'd call home.

Those weeks before filming were exactly what the doctor ordered. I explored the property, a sprawling mass of land, its acreage outnumbered only by the activities it offered. I fell into a routine early. I found favorite restaurants and became a regular at mealtime. I lifted weights at the gym and explored interesting running paths for my early-morning workouts. Most significantly,

I built relationships with the behind-the-scenes staff who kept Nemacolin's gears turning. I fostered friendships with those people who, as the weeks went on, became my sounding board in otherwise lonely times. People like Tim, who, when he saw my energy sinking mid-season, drove an hour and a half back to Pittsburgh to surprise me with a heaping platter of the hot wings we both loved. He had a special kind of generosity that seemed to be shared among the staff at Nemacolin. Co-workers called each other family. They were happy people, grateful to have meaningful work in a corner of the country that might otherwise have gone forgotten.

Ask them the source of their joy, and they all pointed to the same woman—Maggie—the owner of Nemacolin who maestro'd this massive undertaking. Maggie was a boss. We grew close—I ducked away from scheduled events more than once to commiserate with her over a home-cooked meal. I admired Maggie. She commanded a small army of workers with care and kindness and orchestrated a flourishing center of economic activity for the community. When ABC employees erected branding and soundstages across Nemacolin, they did so on land Maggie *owned*. She carried real power, yet wielded it lightly.

I can't stress the importance of these relationships enough. To the contestants and producers, I would be *The Bachelor*. But to Maggie and her people, I was just Matt. During filming, questionable incentives caused some people to act in strange ways. People's behavior swung wildly from pandering to lashing out, depending on what they thought would play best on TV. I counted on Maggie's crew for doses of realness.

Second to Maggie's staff was the advance team that ABC sent to Nemacolin to prepare for the season ahead. They were a small army of people zigzagging the property like bees constructing a hive. Producers, camerapeople, directors, assistants, and other folks whose titles combined all those other titles in complex strands. I found in them the same qualities I found in Nemacolin's staff—generosity, kindness, and warmth. They too delivered reality checks once the season began filming. I cherished those shows of friendship in an otherwise topsy-turvy time.

Whatever mixed feelings I may have about *The Bachelor* franchise after my season, whatever disagreements I may feel with the way I was portrayed or how conversations I remember clearly were ultimately characterized, you will never see me disparage the show publicly. I know personally the faceless mass of people propping up the franchise. They are hardworking and kindhearted friends, relying on a show that employs hundreds for their livelihoods. You don't mess with that.

When filming began, I stepped naïvely into an odd social experiment. I entered the show open to the possibility of finding the love of my life. I didn't count on it, but I thought it possible. So many people told me, in one way or another, how weird it was to turn to a reality show for love. I disagreed—how was it any different than bumping into your soulmate in the produce aisle? Both relied on chance. At least on *The Bachelor*, everyone arrived with the same openness. The odds favored love. And on the first night, gazing at the gorgeous women who had gathered for the same reason I had, it seemed entirely possible that my future fiancée was among the crowd. Then the drama started.

It isn't useful to rehash every skirmish that broke out over the weeks of filming, but they combined to sour the experience. I'm not talking about the genuine emotion that poured out of people, including myself. I deeply appreciated the vulnerability that many women showed. Vulnerability is an act of faith. I felt honored whenever anyone trusted me with their truest self.

I'm talking about the blatantly inauthentic dramatic twists that waited around every corner. "Stay tuned for…" moments. Drama for drama's sake. This is where my unfamiliarity with the franchise's past really handicapped me. I didn't appreciate just how mean-spirited people could get with one another. The calculated conflicts wore on me. I am well-intentioned and try, at all times, to assume best intent in others. I came into the experience promising to be my most authentic self. I quickly grew disillusioned seeing how some others embraced conflict for the sake of new followers or good TV.

Isolation made the politics of the show particularly difficult. When you enter the *Bachelor* bubble, you forfeit contact with the outside world. The network can't have spoilers weaseling their way out. Initially, I embraced the requirement—disconnecting would force me to remain focused on the important process at hand. But giving away my phone also meant sacrificing my support system—Mom, John, Tyler, Kev, Mike, and others—whom I called in crazy times. I didn't appreciate how deeply I relied on them until they were out of reach. Under normal circumstances, they'd counsel me through difficult decisions. In Nemacolin, when faced with difficult decisions almost daily, I had to go on instinct alone. And when times got tough, when my vulnerability collided head-on with my unprocessed trauma, the people who had carried me through past low points were too distant to lend a hand.

Despite the challenges, romance bloomed. Such incredible women traveled to Nemacolin for the season, women who checked all my boxes—kindhearted, ambitious, intelligent, and committed to their families. Our relationships deepened as time progressed. In rare one-on-one moments, I shared stories of my mother—my rock—and the complex men I grew up around. I spoke of the fury I harbored for my father, cooled only by the Christian forgiveness my mother instilled. Of the equal parts fear and pride I felt for John. Of my grandfather—my most complex relationship of all. They reciprocated with their own vulnerabilities, sharing intimacies they'd long tucked away.

One criticism I faced months later, once the season aired, was that I was too bland or boring to anchor a season of *The Bachelor*. Maybe that's true, but it's impossible to know from what was actually aired. I shared honest moments with women who were just as committed to showing their full selves as I was. I exposed my fears, faults, and contradictions for them, and America, to judge. It wasn't easy for any of us, but it was necessary for any chance of love to remain alive. Those moments went unseen.

In a show that gave me access to endless resources—a sprawling resort, dozens of support staff, and too many excursions to name—my most precious asset was time. Early in the process, I wanted to spend all I had with one woman. In the beginning, she cut through the polished front I'd honed and into my nerdy side. We debated who was the bigger fan of *How to Train Your Dragon* and Marvel movies. I observed her empathy from afar, noticed how her kindness extended beyond our time alone and to everyone else she encountered. I listened to how she spoke about her family. Conversations deepened after that. I discussed the troubled legacy I felt I had been handed. I told her about my own reservations about falling in love, for fear of history repeating itself. She cared for my wounds. She exposed hers in return.

I'm often asked if I knew before the finale that I would choose Rachael. The answer is absolutely yes.

I couldn't say that, of course. The season finale had to deliver suspense and surprise. But, stepping to the platform with Rachael in our final moments, it felt like the end was inevitable all along. We concluded the journey the way we experienced it—together.

In our final on-air moments, I shared my heart with Rachael. When I told her I was committed to her, I meant it. When I told her I saw us building a family together, I meant it. And when I told her I loved her, more than any other time I'd used the phrase, I meant that too.

I handed her the final rose, and we floated off the platform together. Of course, neither of us foresaw the shitstorm that awaited.

The first lesson you learn after being announced as the Bachelor is to ignore social media chatter. I stopped checking Instagram, except to post occasionally, and all of my friends knew not to send me the latest gossip. I wasn't interested. With a new "controversy" brewing every day, ignorance was truly bliss. So, when rumors about Rachael began bubbling up in the middle of the season, they took weeks to reach me. First came allegations of high school bullying, then insensitive comments she supposedly made. A TikTok rant about her past circulated on the web. It pulled her parents' voting record into the fray. News leaked that she and I chose each other at the end. The microscope on her life intensified.

Even after filming, *especially* after filming, being the Bachelor was a full-time job. I ran around the country constantly for appearances and interviews, too busy to pay any mind to noisy nonsense about my girlfriend. Rachael and I spoke almost hourly and were as in love as ever. We couldn't be seen in public together until news of our relationship became official so, while I hopped from flight to flight, she returned to Georgia to spend time with her family. She mentioned that some things about her past had popped up on the web, but I shrugged it off and told her not to worry about it. The Twitter mob would have a new target soon enough.

Then the picture dropped.

It found me in my New York apartment. The TV flashed an entertainment news alert with Rachael's face on it. She was done up—long-lashed and powdered cheeks—with a poufy princess dress ruffling down from her shoulders. "BREAKING NEWS" blinked in red. The dress wasn't just any dress, it was an antebellum-styled dress. The photos were taken prior to a Rose Ball Formal at a campus fraternity. An anchorman caught me up on the weeks-long buildup that I'd shut out. Social media stuck disparate puzzle pieces together. The photo was the missing piece that brought the whole concocted image into focus. They declared Rachael a racist.

She called me immediately. I knew the woman I'd chosen to be with. Celebrity gossip, no matter how sensitive, wouldn't shape my opinion of her. We had gone through too much together already. And I knew, in that moment, she'd be hurting.

Her voice on the other end was strained and unsteady. Messages—horrible messages—had poured into her in-box. My only role in that moment was to console her. I assured her that I knew who she was; that this too would pass. I caught the emotions that spilled out of her and tried to provide strength in return. She was a solemn storm.

I still didn't quite understand what kind of crisis we were dealing with. Judging by her tone alone, I knew it wasn't like the other petty nothings that always popped up.

Peeking into the gossip sites once we hung up was like standing before a dam as it was breached. There were more articles than any one man could read. Our names were coupled and plastered across news outlets large and small. The media mob chanted buzzwords in unison: privileged, insensitive, racist.

The days that followed are a blur. My reputation shifted in the minds of many. They questioned my character and judgment. Everyone called me—friends, family, agents, networks. Many were genuinely empathetic. Some were gnats, seeing sweet gossip and eager to feed. Rachael suffered, seeing every past mistake, down to the minute, paraded across headlines. And of course, during that period, the show's host gave one of the worst interviews in modern memory. The scandal escalated. The walls closed in.

Days passed before I had a moment to consider what the revelation meant to me, personally, or what, if anything, it should mean about my relationship with the woman I loved. I retreated to Tyler's place in Florida and used the silence to consider all that had just transpired.

Looking again at the picture, it conjured memories from an earlier life. I remembered my days in middle and high school, once my frame filled out, wrestling with how to move through the world in my Black body. I saw how the world regarded men of my size and complexion, how it moved away in fear. I compensated early in life. I took pains to appear nonthreatening, dedicating myself to a sport and flashing polished smiles at the parents when they approached. I wanted the world to embrace me, and from the time I hit my growth spurt, I felt like I was working against my own biology to earn that warmth. I did it, though. I became Mr. Sanderson, the likeable football standout whom you were proud to bring home to Mom and Dad.

I remembered how none of that mattered once I entered college. Wake Forest was a new world, and it didn't know me from Adam. I was another six-foot-something Black man with dreads, and that was all most people needed to know. A night out for Kev and me meant rejection, rejection, rejection: stepping to frat houses and watching frat boys eye us, but not see us, before slamming the door shut. I'd spent my life attempting to win favor for the man, the individual, I was. But individuality was useless in a world where my race defined me.

Looking at the picture of Rachael, I wondered where I would have fit at that party. Then I answered my own question: I wouldn't have.

The picture forced deeper realizations about our relationship as well. Rachael and I had hardly talked about race.

Throughout the show, we discussed the things we had in common—cartoons and superheroes, but also family and values. Those shared qualities became the foundation of our relationship, our love. I talked about Blackness often during filming, but almost exclusively with the Black women who had come to Nemacolin. That, of course, was for the same reason—we shared in Blackness and grew close over it.

Race arose only once between Rachael and me. Late in the season, the number of contestants dwindled, and we imagined life after filming for the two of us. She asked if I was prepared for the backlash we'd face, a mixed-race couple formed before America. I see now that she asked one question, but I responded to another. She had in her mind the white Southerners that she knew well. I considered the many Black people who would feel betrayed.

Even if we had been on the same page, my answer would have been the same. None of it mattered. What mattered was how we felt about each other. Our love could withstand temporary judgment.

I was naïve. I didn't anticipate just how divisive we would become. But more than the external perception, I didn't recognize the role that race would play between the two of us. I am many things—a son, a brother, a man of God—and my race is just as formative a force as all those other traits. I am Black. My partner would need to understand that—not just the fact of my race, but also its many implications. Rachael and I had committed to each other without ever exploring one of my most central traits. And if that had gone unexplored, what else could be lingering out there with the potential to divide us?

I needed to see Rachael's face for the hard conversation ahead.

I flew to Georgia for Valentine's Day. We still couldn't be seen in public together, so I arranged a house for us to meet in middle-of-nowhere Georgia, away from her hometown. We called these random locations "safe houses," poking fun at the incognito life we led, but jumping through hoops to see my own girlfriend had long lost its charm by then.

Butterflies crept through my insides on the drive to the safe house. I hadn't felt so nervous to see Rachael since handing her the final rose. We'd come a long way, even since then, but there was a formalness to our meeting this time that felt unfamiliar and uneasy.

We hugged when I arrived. She and I spent two days together, and then on the third day we had the hard conversation. I shared how it felt seeing her, a woman I loved, embody a role that had once so antagonized me. My emotions welled up, and she met me at their peak. She leaned forward and dove in. She'd only been in the sorority a short time; she left the semester following the party. She didn't know about the context of the party when she chose to attend; it was just another college event in her mind. She didn't offer her ignorance as an excuse. Just a fact—she paired it with the facts of her remorse and regret. Tears streamed down both our faces. She apologized for the pain I felt. I forgave her.

Upon returning home to Tyler's in Florida, I knew we needed to step away from each other for a time. Rachael and I had been on an accelerated track since the show began. In a matter of weeks, we jumped from strangers to madly in love. We discussed children and lives together. And I didn't regret a single second of any of it. But, presented with this new information, I needed to slow the train down. We both needed to reflect on the relationship we'd developed; to ask ourselves how deep its roots really reached. And she needed time to understand the Black experience; to "do the work." For her own sake, but also to give our love a chance to be maintained.

Rachael and I didn't speak for a couple of weeks after the Valentine's Day trip. Anyone who has ever been through a breakup can relate to the strangeness of being in constant contact with someone one moment, then cutting it off cold-turkey the next. I'd grown used to our regular check-ins, the gratification of her FaceTimes, seeing her smiling face. Weeks without it felt like dancing off-beat. Both of us knew the silence couldn't last forever, though. We marked our calendars for mid-March. That was when the After the Final Rose ceremony, the grand finale that reunited me with all the women from our season, was scheduled. Rachael broke our silence a week before the reunion, and we texted every day thereafter. We still had feelings for each other, though we didn't know what to do with them. We decided to keep talking, to be open to our love building back.

After the Final Rose was bizarre. We'd spent such an intense time lumped together. But it had been weeks since all that had concluded. Things changed during our time in the open air, away from the *Bachelor* bubble. We'd grown in different ways through the experience and brought our new, improved selves to the studio. Gone were the forced smiles and fluttered eyelashes once glued to the women I'd met. I wasn't a prize, and they weren't contestants. We could be honest now. More than one felt hurt by how I had handled things. If they did, they told me clearly. They were frustrated, relieved, and plenty else. They presented their most authentic selves. I respected and appreciated the bluntness. Michelle and Katie became Bachelorettes that night. I mean this next part wholeheartedly: I wish them all nothing but the best. They deserve happiness, and I hope they find it.

I returned a changed man as well, and one obvious change raised eyebrows. I sported a bushy, unruly beard that I've kept ever since. Being the Bachelor came with pressures and discomforts that I wanted to stuff into the past. The beard felt like a symbol of my old life returning. Out was the clean-cut Matt who felt he had to be Mr. America. I could be myself again.

Things felt strangest between Rachael and me. We hadn't seen each other since Georgia a month prior, but we'd talked a lot in the lead-up to the episode. As far as most of America was concerned, our relationship was still frozen in the blissful moment when I handed her the final rose, but so much had happened since then. So the entire conversation between us felt like it was in service of the viewers, rather than each other. We caught people up. We remained noncommittal. We spoke in cold, curt sentences. But when the cameras shut off, we strode hand-in-hand back to the green room. We both still felt the spark. We took the rare opportunity to speak face-to-face and agreed to keep working on us.

I returned to bouncing around the country on a post-*Bachelor* tour. New York, LA, Miami in a dizzying loop, with other cities sprinkled in between. Rachael and I still had plenty of work left to do. There were many FaceTimes after AFR. Nightly. For hours. There were uncertainty, understanding, and an ultimatum. I took advantage of our undefined, gray space and reconnected with former flings. I knew I had something special with Rachael and thought we might soon come back together. I wanted to make sure I didn't still have lingering feelings for others I'd known before taking that step. It was a mistake. Rachael got wind and was justifiably hurt and feeling betrayed. "I know we're not together right now, but I thought we were building toward something. You need to decide if that is what you want or not. I won't be just another girl you're talking to." After that, there was silence. More painful silence. She stormed out of my life for the last time, I thought.

One weekend in April, I flew to Atlanta to watch influencers punch each other. Triller, the video-sharing social network, hosted a boxing match and invited me to sit ringside for the action. Working out in the hotel gym the morning before the fight, I received a pinging notification on my phone: "Rachael Kirkconnell is now sharing her location with you." I was confused; we hadn't spoken in two long weeks. I checked her pin. She was two blocks away. Was this some kind of cryptic message? I didn't want to miss an opportunity to see her. I rushed over to her red dot on the map and FaceTimed her when I arrived.

Turns out, she hadn't meant to send the notification at all; she didn't even know I was in Atlanta. She had just unblocked my contact, which triggered the location sharing to return automatically—a crazy coincidence that felt fated. I asked if we could talk. She told me we had nothing to talk about. I pleaded, coaxed, and convinced. She relented. We met in the parking garage in her car, far from the public eye. We talked for four hours in that car about all of the issues that had kept us apart—her mistakes, my mistakes, insecurities, family drama, public perception, and everything else under the sun. I decided to be better going forward. She had done self-work that I hadn't reciprocated. I promised her that I was all in. It was the best decision I could have made.

We both are still adjusting to life after the show. The height of the public scrutiny has (hopefully) passed, but some elements of fame never quite settle into place. I miss wandering around New York aimlessly, following my nose into lunch spots. I miss the wonder I first felt at the city, the sense of its limitless heights. You see yourself enough times in unexpected paparazzi photos and begin to suspect you're always being watched. I miss the freedom of anonymity.

Would I do it all over again? I would. As crazy as life has become, I like the man I am today. I know to thank the show for some part of that. I changed. I grew. I learned about myself, my past trauma, and my capacity for love. I learned my breaking point exists somewhere past the horizon. I learned to kiss with my eyes closed.

And the platform it provided has enabled me to discover new

passions to invest in. It's brought me into orbit with other passionate people on the cutting edge of their fields.

ABC Food Tours has taken on a new life. We continue to take kids on tours across New York, but the recent attention has caused me to refocus the mission of the nonprofit. Feeding kids healthy food is the driving force behind all we do. That purpose led me down unexpected alleyways. I'm a deep believer in hydroponic farming—the vertical, indoor growing system that looks like how astronauts might farm on the space station. Here's a sustainable, low-cost, low-maintenance way to grow organic fruits and veggies in a few square feet of space; it was an answer to all the many problems I saw in the food system in New York. As importantly, it's proven to be a great teaching tool for kids hungry to learn where their food comes from. I'm all in on hydroponics and looking forward to the day when every community has its own set of growing systems to feed and teach.

I've made one other big bet on the future: cryptocurrency. There too, my mission to empower underserved communities led me to thrilling new territory. When the Bitcoin craze struck, hobby investors across the country rushed to crypto like digital gold. The underlying technology—blockchain—piqued my interest. Its decentralized system will democratize banking. Soon, low-income communities will obtain financing without jumping through the hoops imposed by traditional banks and gatekeepers. Thanks to the platform the show granted me, I've been allowed a seat alongside the men and women revolutionizing the way we think about financing.

I hit a major mile marker recently: thirty years old. Hard to believe I've grown so...elderly.

I reflect back on my first thirty years of life with amazement. No one would have looked at me, a twiggy nineties baby with too much energy and too little attention span, and predicted all that the future would have in store. I live a life today that I couldn't have conjured up in my wildest prayers.

Lord willing, I have a lot of life left. If the first thirty years were any indication, the next thirty will be an incredible ride. The lessons I've learned thus far I'll carry with me. Plus, I'll save a little room for all the new ones yet to come.

Acknowledgments

First Impressions could only have come together by God's grace.

Mom, this achievement is yours even more than it is my own. With nothing but determination, faith, and love, you singlehandedly turned two boys into men. I'm proud of you, just as I know you are of me. Thank you for giving me the best parts of yourself and teaching me how to seek out the rest. I love you.

John, my brother, we were born to be best friends. You've overcome more than most, and no one is prouder of you than I am. Continue along your path, striving for the best of life. There's no one I'd rather spend life alongside.

Ms. Cameron, thank you for pushing me to reach for unknowable possibilities. I wish you were here to see how far we've come. I know you're looking down smiling.

Tyler, Gucci Shane, KJ, Mike, Jackson, Kobby, Grace, Hannah—y'all are the family I chose. I couldn't have made it through this journey without your endless support and care. I hope to always be as good a friend to you as you all are to me.

Cole, you killed it.

Mr. Dixon, Hampton, Haley, and the whole WME team, your expertise continues to guide me through the uncharted worlds of television, publishing, sponsorships, and so much more. Thank you for always treating me like family and having my back when I don't know any better.

Karen, Morgan, Catherine, and all the folks at Hachette, thank you for trusting me to tell my story my way and for shepherding this project from first draft to final.

And to the Bachelor Nation fans who have supported me through months and months of ups, downs, and in-betweens, thank you from the bottom of my heart. Stepping into your world was the joy I did not know I needed. Your continued generosity keeps a smile on my face every day.

About the Author

Matt James is an American television personality, philanthropist, and entrepreneur who was the first Black Bachelor in the popular series' twenty-five-season history. Today, Matt continues to lead his nonprofit, ABC Food Tours, which has exposed thousands of kids across New York to nutrition education. He is also an investor, acting on the leading edge of hydroponic farming and the cryptocurrency revolution.

Cole Brown is a political commentator, writer, and author of the book *Greyboy: Finding Blackness in a White World*. *Greyboy* received an NAACP Image Award nomination for Outstanding Literary Work—Debut Author and was selected for Steph Curry's "Underrated" book club. Today, Cole lives between Los Angeles and New York working on various film and literary projects.